J.S. Bach's

FIFTEEN TWO-PART
INVENTIONS FOR GUITAR

Master all 15 of J.S. Bach's Inventions With Live-Recorded Duet Backing Tracks

LEVI**CLAY**

FUNDAMENTAL**CHANGES**

J.S. Bach's Fifteen Two-Part Inventions For Guitar

Master all 15 of J.S. Bach's Inventions With Live-Recorded Duet Backing Tracks

ISBN: 978-1-78933-470-8

Published by **www.fundamental-changes.com**

Copyright © 2025 Levi Clay

Edited by Joseph Alexander

www.fundamental-changes.com

Join our free Facebook Community of Cool Musicians

www.facebook.com/groups/fundamentalguitar

For over 350 free guitar lessons with Videos, check out:

www.fundamental-changes.com

Cover Image Copyright: Luis Orozco at Gepettos Guild Guitars

www.gepettosguild.com

Contents

Chapter One – Introduction and History

Few composers in history are as revered as Johann Sebastian Bach. Born in Germany in 1685, Bach is one of the defining figures of the Baroque era. With more than 1,100 compositions written for a wide range of instruments and ensembles, his music continues to be studied in schools and performed by passionate societies across the world, centuries after his death.

Bach's work is a masterclass in melody, counterpoint, modulation, and more. From the grandeur of the orchestral Brandenburg Concertos and choral Masses to solo masterpieces like the Goldberg Variations, Cello Suites, and Violin Partitas, his output is vast and influential.

Many of Bach's most studied pieces were written for keyboard instruments like the harpsichord, clavichord, and organ. Though he was familiar with the early fortepiano, the modern piano as we know it wasn't something Bach encountered. The same goes for the guitar, as he didn't write specifically for it, although he did compose music for the lute, which offers some crossover.

Often, Bach marked his keyboard works as being "for clavier," simply meaning any type of keyboard. His famous Well-Tempered Clavier is a standout example.

In this book, we focus on his Fifteen Two-Part Inventions. Originally written as a keyboard study book for his son Wilhelm Friedemann Bach, these works later became staple teaching pieces for his students.

I often used the Inventions in my formative years, as sight-reading studies. Despite being keyboard music, the Inventions aren't chordal. Instead, they are contrapuntal, with two independent lines flowing simultaneously. While keyboard players are tasked with playing both parts at once, we'll be treating them as duets for two guitars.

These Inventions are commonly paired with the Sinfonias, which extend the ideas to three-part counterpoint. Those would suit three-guitar arrangements, but they were too much to fit into a single book. If you're new to Bach, this collection is a great place begin, however, Bach's catalogue is vast, and I encourage you to dig deeper.

Since Bach predates recording technology, there's always an element of interpretation when playing his music. Different musicians bring their own character to his work, which is why it's valuable to listen to multiple recordings of the same piece. Pianists such as András Schiff and Glenn Gould each bring distinct personalities to their interpretations. Some purists may raise their eyebrows, but I find their insights fascinating.

For the recordings in this book, I played everything straight and to a click track, so you can practice along easily. In a perfect world, I'd use rubato to add more expressive phrasing. However, a strict tempo brings its own challenge, which I hope you'll enjoy.

I've also provided recordings of each hand in isolation, along with full performances both with and without a click. This gives you the option to study each part closely, or even play along with me to create the feeling that we're performing together.

Finally, a quick note that these pieces are not organised in order of difficulty and some are much easier than others, so explore the book and listen to the audio before picking your first study piece. I recommend starting with Invention Fifteen, then Nine, then Seven.

Get the Audio

The audio files for this book are available to download for free from **www.fundamental-changes.com.** The link is in the top right-hand corner. Click on the "Guitar" link then simply select this book title from the drop-down menu and follow the instructions to get the audio.

We recommend that you download the files directly to your computer (not to your tablet or phone) and extract them there before adding them to your media library. If you encounter any difficulty, we provide technical support within 24 hours via the contact form.

For over 350 free guitar lessons with videos check out:

www.fundamental-changes.com

Join our free Facebook Community of Cool Musicians

www.facebook.com/groups/fundamentalguitar

Tag us for a share on Instagram: **FundamentalChanges**

Chapter Two – From Keyboard to Guitar!

When I began working on these pieces as part of my own practice, I quickly saw their potential as the foundation for a book. After arranging a few, it felt like a natural project to dive into. So you can imagine my frustration when I discovered that other authors had already published books on the same idea. I bought a few to see how they stacked up, and the fact that you're reading this one probably tells you everything you need to know. They didn't even come close to what they needed to be.

Despite claiming to be accurate transcriptions of Bach's music, many of these arrangements overlook a crucial point. The guitar is an octave-transposing instrument, which means the music we read sounds an octave lower than written.

It's far easier to visualise this on a piano. Take "middle C" for example. On a keyboard, it's played here:

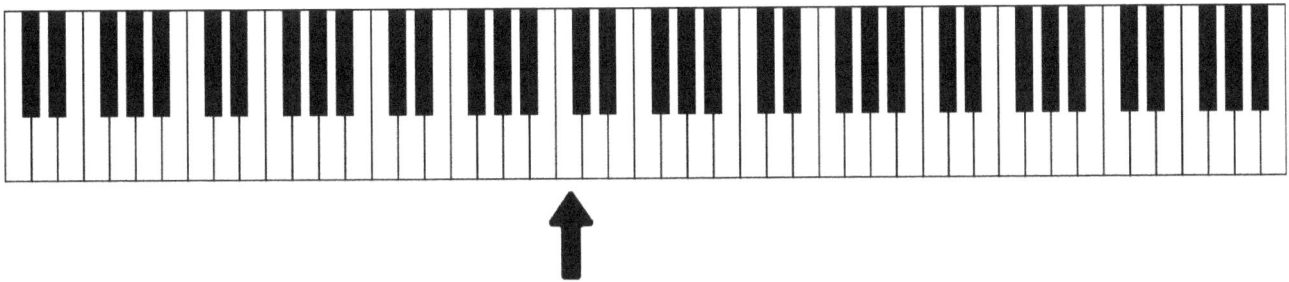

But when you play a written middle C on the guitar, the actual pitch you hear is this:

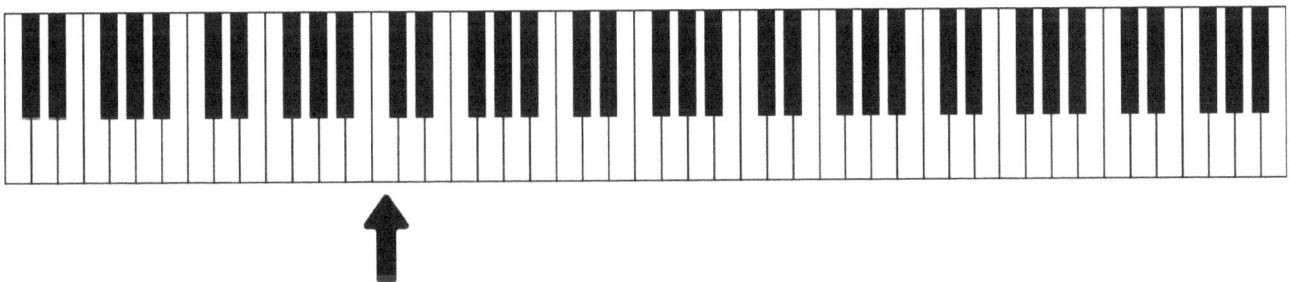

This has serious implications when arranging music that wasn't originally written for guitar. If we want to honour the composer's intent, we need to compensate for the octave drop by playing the music an octave higher than written. Otherwise, the balance between the two parts is lost, especially in contrapuntal music like this.

Many arrangements I've seen fall into the trap of simply importing MIDI files into notation software and printing whatever the computer generates. This completely misses Bach's carefully crafted register separation between left and right hands. You can see what he intended visually on the keyboard below.

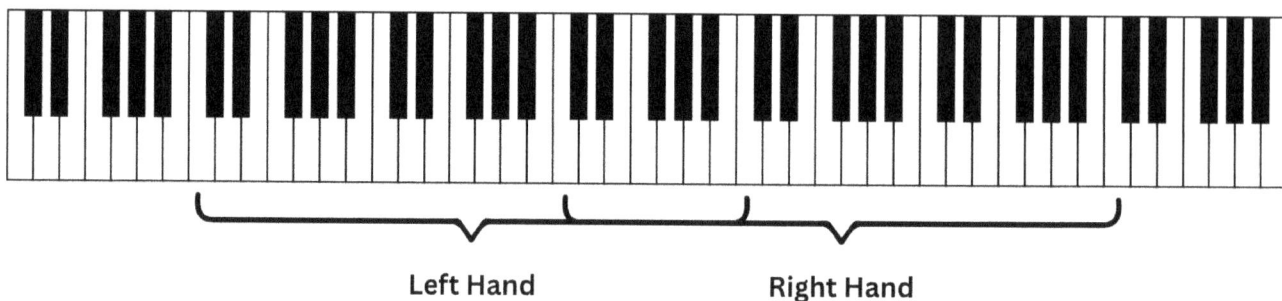

Left Hand   Right Hand

As you can see, there's often a small area of crossover between the hands in these pieces, but typically the left hand plays in its lower register, while the right hand occupies its own higher space. If you don't transpose the right hand part, you end up with the following range, which creates a muddled texture and doesn't emphasise the part separation. It might make the pieces easier to play, but it forces both parts into the same range and goes against Bach's musical intention.

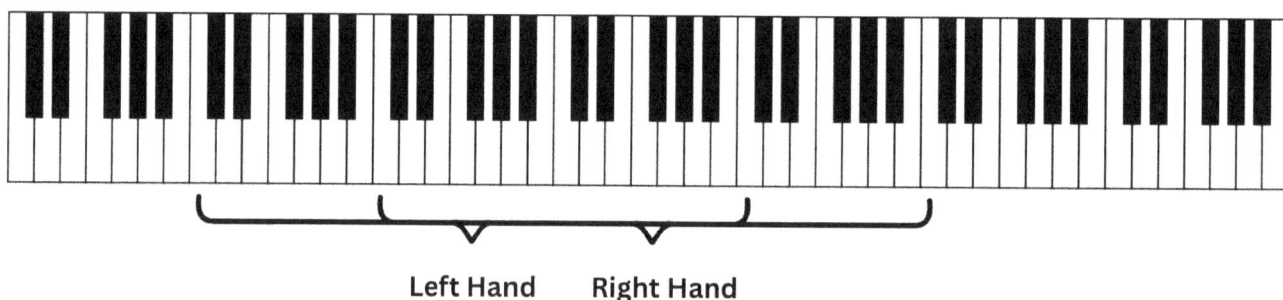

Left Hand   Right Hand

In this book, we'll take the right-hand parts further up the neck to maintain their proper register. Nothing goes beyond the 20th fret on the high E string, and playing this high up only happens occasionally.

I also was surprised to see other books claiming to be faithful to Bach's original compositions, especially when the left hand (accompanying bass part) in every single Invention drops below the range of a standard six-string guitar. I wanted to stay as close as possible to the source material, so to solve this problem I wrote the left-hand parts for seven-string guitar.

Before you slam this book closed in disgust, let me be clear! In most cases, only a few notes fall below the pitch of the low E string, and you can easily adapt these parts for six-string guitar if needed. But I wanted to give you the most accurate version possible, so I recorded both parts using my seven-string Ibanez Archtop, which I strung with a custom set of D'Addario flat-wound strings of gauges 15, 17, 24, 32, 42, 52, 75.

My suggestion is to begin by learning the right-hand (melody) parts of each piece and have me accompany you on the backing tracks with the full-range seven-string bass part. If you're curious about trying seven-string yourself, you can. If not, you can simply shift any written low Cs, Ds, and the occasional B up an octave.

I've ensured that the fingerings shown in the tablature are arranged as an actual guitarist would play. And the proof is in the recording, as I am playing these arrangements for real. That might sound obvious, but you'd be surprised. I picked up a few other books while working on this and one of them used MIDI playback as the audio. The fingerings had been thrown together with so little care, it was obvious that the author hadn't actually played the music at all.

Take your time learning the arrangements. Break them down into small phrases and increase your speed gradually. Remember that these pieces were written for the keyboard, so some parts are naturally more challenging to play on guitar.

Each Invention comes with six audio files, so use these to your advantage!

I've included,

- Both parts played with a click

- Both parts played without a click

- Right hand played with a click

- Right hand played without a click

- Left hand played with a click

- Left hand played without a click

When learning the right-hand part, start by listening with a click to hear how the rhythm locks in with the beat. Be precise. There's no room for guesswork here, as later you'll be playing with the accompaniment, so your timing needs to be solid.

When you're confident, try playing the right-hand part over the left-hand backing track – first with a click, then without.

Finally, you might want to learn the left-hand part too. As mentioned, these will need small adjustments if you're playing a six-string, but they're no more difficult than the right-hand parts. In fact, you might even find them more enjoyable, as they sit in a more accessible part of the neck.

Chapter Three – Scale Primer

Before getting fully stuck into these studies, I thought it would be useful to include a short chapter on scales and technique. These pieces were originally written to help keyboard players build control and fluency, especially when writing in a wide range of keys. There are 15 inventions in this book, each in a different key, so having a few reliable scale fingerings under your belt will really help.

That said, it's not just about staying in one key.

Bach was a master of modulation, and his music moves between keys in a way that feels completely natural. None of the inventions remain in a single key from start to finish. Instead, they flow between major and relative minor, or shift to closely related keys e.g., up a fifth to the dominant (for example, from C Major to G Major), or up a fourth to the subdominant (like moving from C Major to F Major).

It can feel like a winding journey, but Bach always brings you home.

I bring this up because recognising these key changes helps you understand what's going on in the music. Rather than trying to memorise every individual note, it's far easier to think, "We start in C, move to G, then into a phrase in E Minor."

Of course, this book isn't designed to cover theory or technique in depth. If you want to go deeper into scale work, I'd recommend checking out my *Guided Guitar Scale Practice Routines* book. That will give you a more complete foundation.

The major scale is a familiar sound throughout these inventions. To get you started, here are four of the fingerings I often use to play a C Major scale.

Example 3a:

You're not likely to come across a simple ascending or descending scale in Bach's music. Instead, you'll often find long, flowing sequences that move within a scale pattern in more interesting ways.

Here's an example from Invention One, where the sequence plays four descending notes, followed by two ascending diatonic thirds, and then repeats the idea.

Example 3b:

When playing in a Major key, Bach often modulated up a 5th to the dominant key. For example, from C Major to G Major. These keys are closely related, so the shift feels natural. You're only introducing one new accidental, which in this case is F#.

C Major:

C D E F G A B C

G Major

G A B C D E F# G

The sudden introduction of F#s in the notation is a giveaway that we've moved to the key of G Major.

Example 3c:

Another option would be to move up a fourth to the subdominant, so from C Major to F Major. Again, there's only a one note difference between the two keys.

F Major

F G A Bb C D E F

So the inclusion of a Bb is the clue that we've shifted keys into F Major.

Example 3d:

A deeper understanding of this subject comes from learning the Circle of Fifths and how key signatures work. That takes time to absorb, and this book isn't meant to be a full theory course. But if it's something you've already explored, I'd encourage you to use that knowledge as you work through these pieces. Don't just copy the TAB, take a moment to consider why you're playing the notes you're seeing.

If you do want to explore this further, here's a basic checklist to focus on:

• Learn the order the keys are arranged in. I recommend starting with the anticlockwise direction on the Circle of Fifths.

• Understand how many accidentals each key has. With each step around the circle, one more is added.

• Learn to read key signatures, so you know that two flats indicates Bb Major, three sharps is A Major, five sharps is B Major, four flats is Ab Major, and so on.

Minor Scales

Each major scale has a relative minor which begins on its 6th degree.

So if we take C Major:

C D E F G A B C

The 6th note is A, and beginning a new scale there creates the A Natural Minor scale:

A B C D E F G A

While Bach occasionally used the natural minor scale, you'd more often hear the distinctive sound of the harmonic minor scale. This is simply the natural minor with the 7th note raised by semitone (half-step).

A Harmonic Minor becomes:

A B C D E F G# A

The fingerings for the harmonic minor scale can be a bit trickier, as you'll sometimes end up with four notes on a string. Here are a few fingerings for A Harmonic Minor to get you started.

Example 3e:

Just as with the Major scales, we can modulate to minor keys too. This is shown clearly in the following example, which moves from C Major to A Minor.

Example 3f:

One of the most important techniques to get comfortable with when playing these pieces is the shift slide. This isn't like a regular legato slide where you pick one note then slide to the next. A shift slide involves picking both notes and fretting them with the same finger.

For example, let's ascend through six notes, then shift from the 8th fret to the 10th using the little finger. After that, you'll descend in the new position before shifting from the 6th fret down to the 5th with the index finger, then repeat the pattern.

Example 3g:

We'll be using this technique throughout the pieces to move smoothly up and down the neck, but effective guitar fingering is not set in stone. You might find that different fingerings suit your hands better, and that's completely fine. Experiment with other approaches and see what works best for you. After all, experimentation is the mother of Invention!

Chapter Four – Technique Primer

I revisited these Inventions in my own practice long before I ever planned to write about them. Partly because I've always had a real fondness for this music and still find it deeply rewarding to play, but also because I wanted to sharpen up my alternate picking technique.

There are a few different opinions about what alternate picking actually *is*. Some players define it as simply alternating down and up strokes with each note. That definition works fine in certain situations, but in my view, it misses the broader picture, especially when the rhythms become more varied.

That strict down-up method works well when you're playing a constant run of 1/16th notes, like this:

Example 4a:

But the trouble starts when the rhythm becomes more varied. In this example, the picking hand still alternates down and up strokes, but I wouldn't consider it true alternate picking.

Example 4b:

In my view, alternate picking is all about the continuous, consistent motion of the picking hand, whether you're striking a note or not.

I like to think of the picking hand as a small motor that keeps turning at a steady pace. So rather than slowing down when you move from 1/16th notes to 1/8th notes, like this:

Example 4c:

You keep the hand moving as if you're still playing 1/16th notes. That means the 1/8th notes are played with downstrokes, and your picking hand doesn't need to shift into a different "gear". This consistency helps your timing stay rock solid.

Example 4d:

With this approach, whenever you're playing within a 1/16th note framework, the downbeats will always land on downstrokes and the upbeats on upstrokes, no matter what the phrase looks like.

This takes time to develop, but once it becomes automatic, your timekeeping and control will improve noticeably.

Here's Example 4b again, this time played with true alternate motion.

Example 4e:

If a phrase doesn't begin on the downbeat, you'll start it with an upstroke instead. You can see this clearly at the beginning of Invention Thirteen.

Example 4f:

This idea can be taken even further. Invention Six places the melody entirely on the off-beats, which makes perfect sense once you realise that the left-hand part is holding down the downbeats.

Example 4g:

If you stick with this approach, you'll likely notice a big improvement in your arpeggio playing. It might feel awkward at first, but it offers far more precision and control than trying to sweep through these kinds of passages.

Example 4h:

You might notice the occasional spot where I bend the rules a little, and that's absolutely fine. Rules are there to guide us, but now and then, breaking them helps the music flow more naturally. When I do that, it's coming from a strong technical foundation, not from avoiding the technique.

For example, in the first Invention, you'll find a two-string sweep in bar six. That small adjustment lets me keep the 1/16th notes flowing with consistent alternate motion.

Another technical challenge across these pieces is the range of the neck. As you move higher up, the frets get smaller and the need for precision increases. On top of that, upper fret access can be limited, especially on certain guitars. I recorded all of these on a 20-fret archtop jazz guitar. The cutaway only gives partial access, and the guitar body is quite thick, so keeping my thumb behind the neck up there just isn't an option.

So, we adapt and overcome!

Sometimes that means using the ring finger instead of the little finger. One finger per fret is useful in exercises, but here we're playing real music, and that means being flexible. If using fingers 1, 2, and 3 at the 17th fret gets the job done more cleanly than trying to squeeze in finger 4, then go with that.

Remember to care about the sound and don't get bogged down in guitar technique "dogma". Listen with your ears, not your eyes, and if it sounds good, then it is good. Be honest with yourself. Does the passage sound the way you want it to? Are you playing with confidence? Is your rhythm locked in?

I believe anyone can make real progress with time and effort. Remember, Bach wrote these inventions as intermediate-level studies for keyboard players who had to play both parts at once. These will be a challenge, but a fun and rewarding one. I believe in you!

Invention One in C Major

For each Invention in this book, I'll share a few thoughts to help guide your study, along with one standout idea that you can take away and work into your own playing. Bach's first Invention is a perfect starting point for anyone wishing to explore counterpoint.

Notice that when one voice plays 1/16th notes, the other often plays 1/8th notes, and to help keep the lines feeling independent, I like to play those 1/8th notes with a short, staccato touch. It gives the parts more clarity, and it's an approach I use throughout the whole book.

Another thing to listen for is how the lower voice often echoes the melody played by the top voice, usually an octave lower. This creates a lovely call-and-response effect and gives the piece a feeling that's almost like a round.

Example 5a:

My favourite lick in this Invention appears in bar three. It features a descending sequence built on fourths, followed by a series of ascending diatonic thirds.

Example 5b:

This idea can be applied to any pattern or key. For example, here's the same basic concept, but this time using the C Minor scale.

Example 5c:

Now here's the full Invention, with the left- and right-hand parts shown together, so you can study how the two voices interact throughout.

Example 5d:

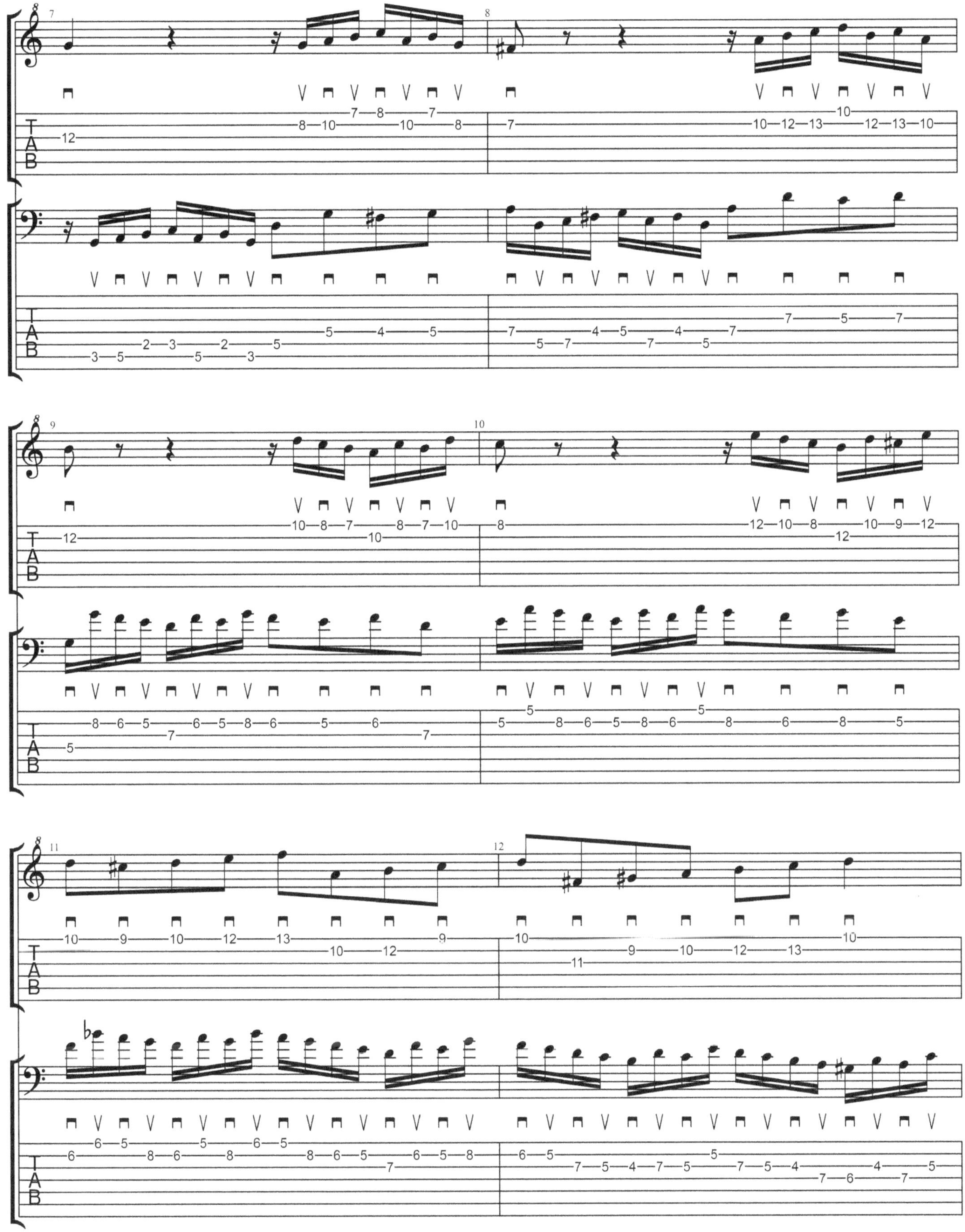

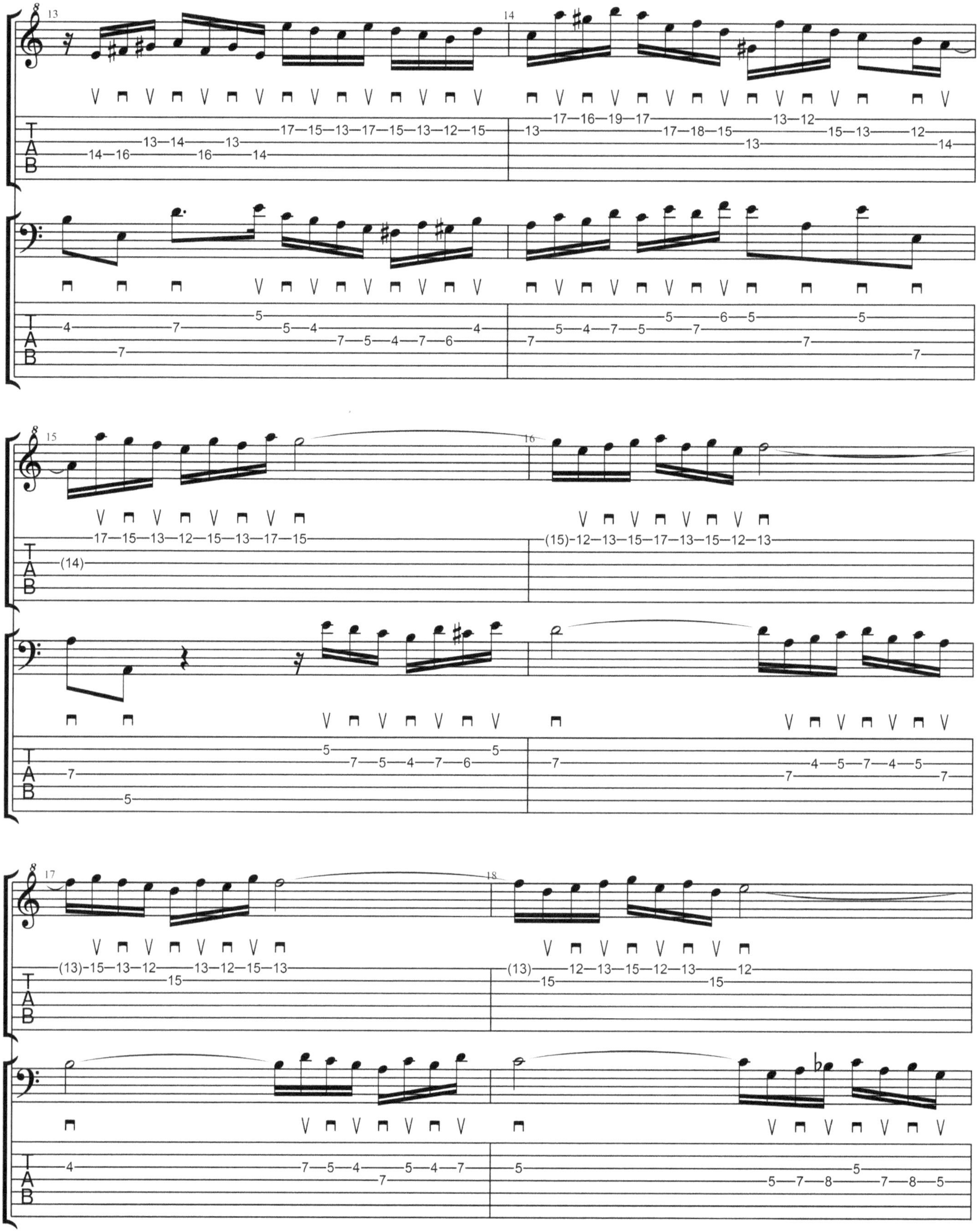

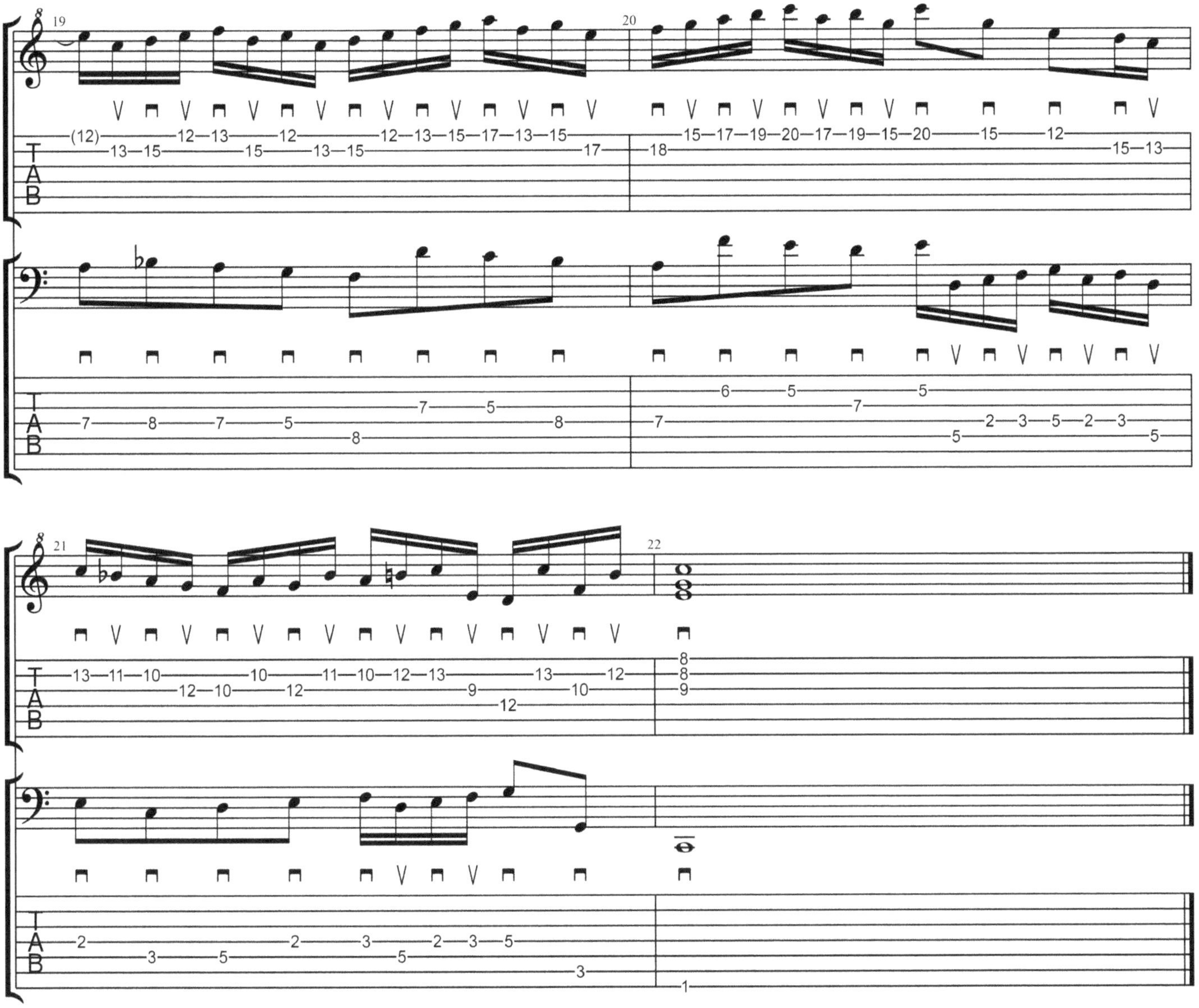

Invention Two in C Minor

The second Invention gives us our first taste of playing in a minor key and is a great example of how Bach combines elements from both the harmonic and natural minor scales.

In the key of C Minor, we expect to have Bb as the b7 degree of C Natural Minor, and B natural as the raised 7th of C Harmonic Minor, and indeed you'll hear both in the very first bar beginning with C, B, C (from the harmonic minor), then switching back to Bb (natural minor) in the second half of the bar.

Another interesting feature of this invention is the use of trills – a form of ornamentation that lets you bring some personal expression to the performance.

Early music often included ornaments like trills, turns, mordents and appoggiaturas. If you're interested in playing Baroque music in a way that reflects the style of the time, these are worth exploring. That said, if you listen to different recordings of these pieces, you'll notice just how much variation there is from one player to the next. My suggestion would be to learn the notes cleanly first, then begin adding embellishments once you feel more confident.

I've included trills in this Invention, so you can hear how they might be used once you've spent some time with the material.

Now, let's look at my favourite phrase in the piece, a lovely combination of an ascending triad followed by a descending scale, all rooted in the key of C Minor.

Example 6a:

For fun, I've taken this idea and applied it to a C Major Scale, descending through each chord in the key and moving across different string sets. It's a beautifully musical exercise to practice and one that you can easily adapt to any scale to create new challenges and variations.

Example 6b:

Now here's the Invention played in its entirety.

Example 6c:

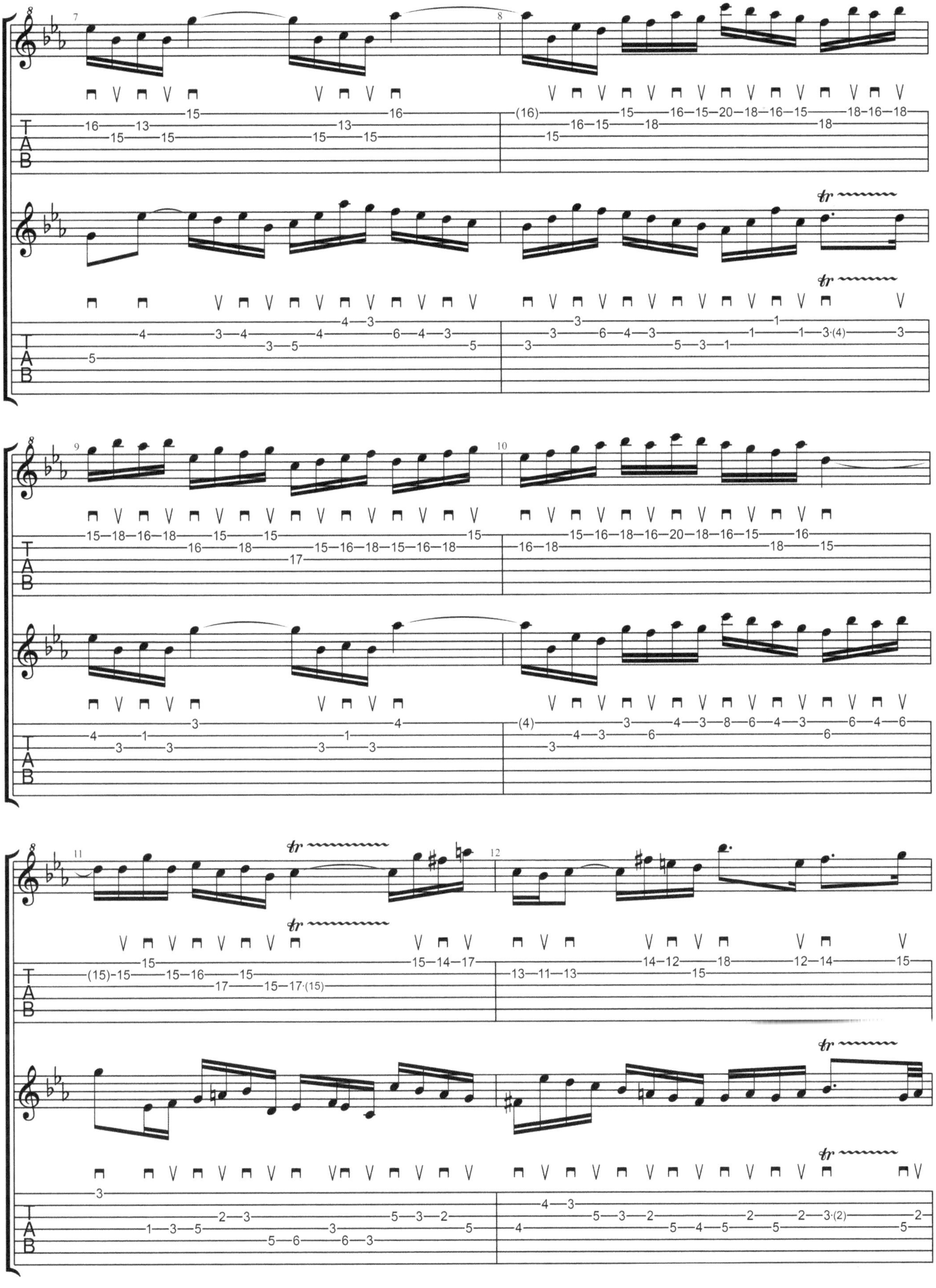

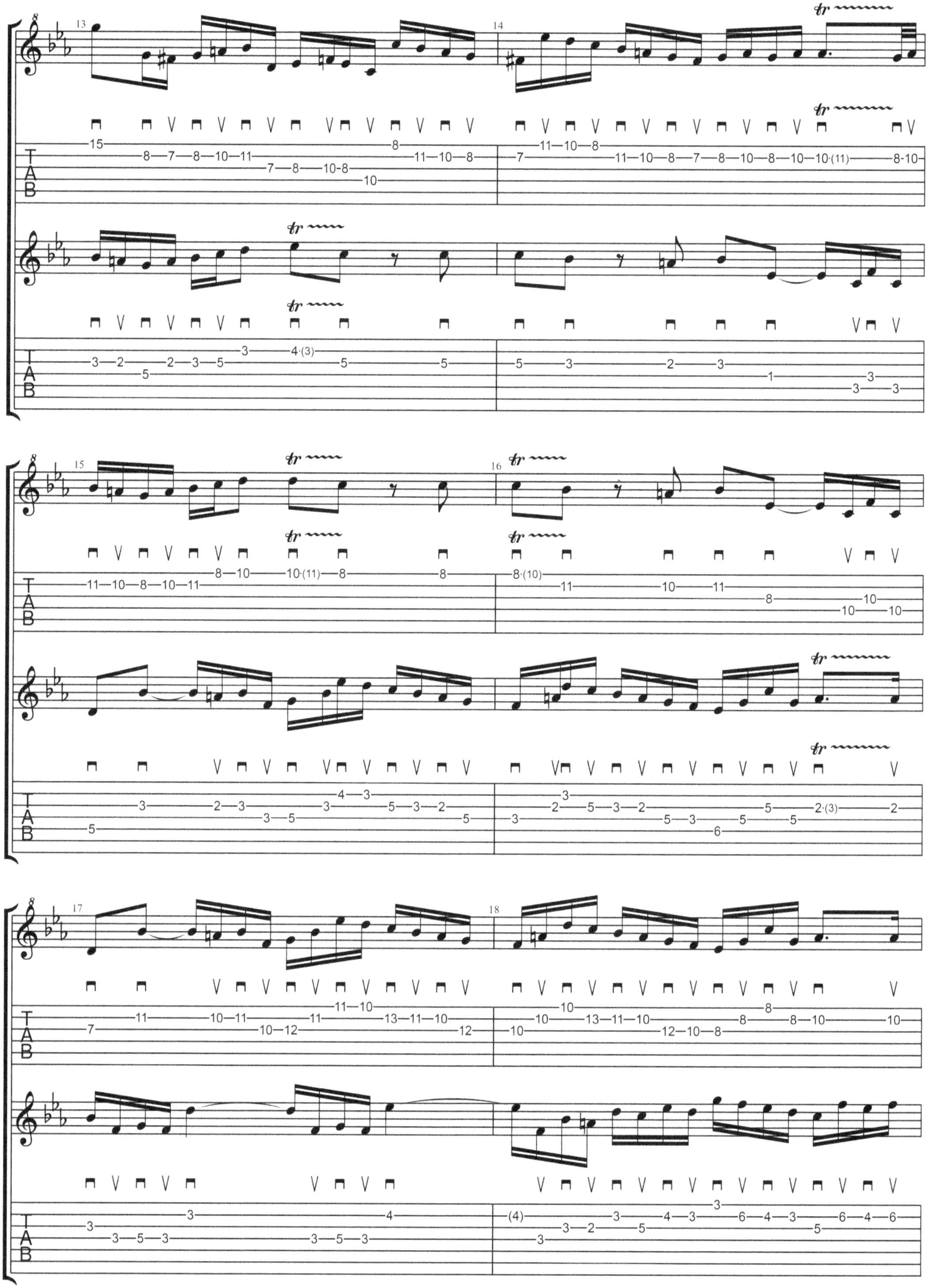

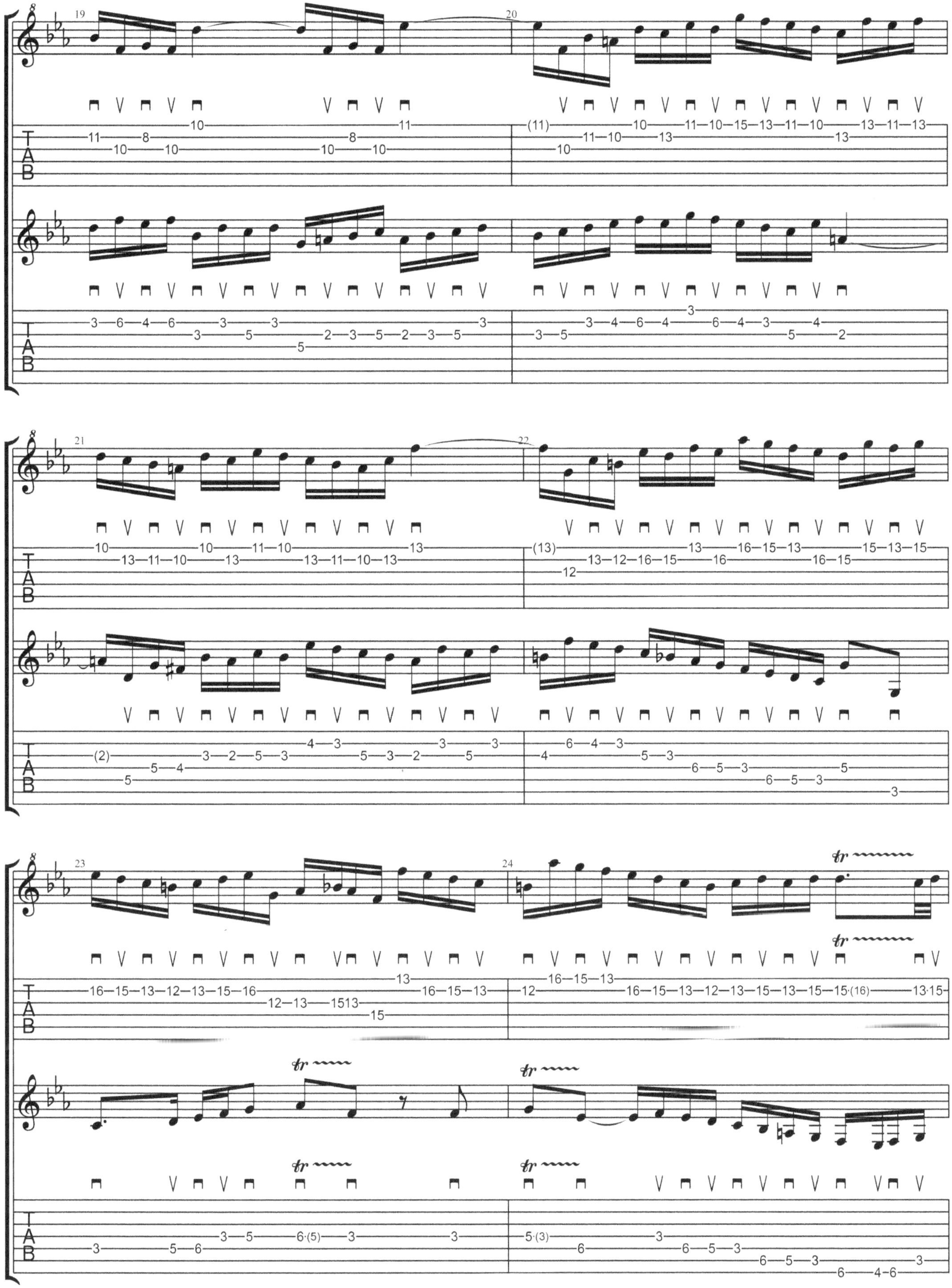

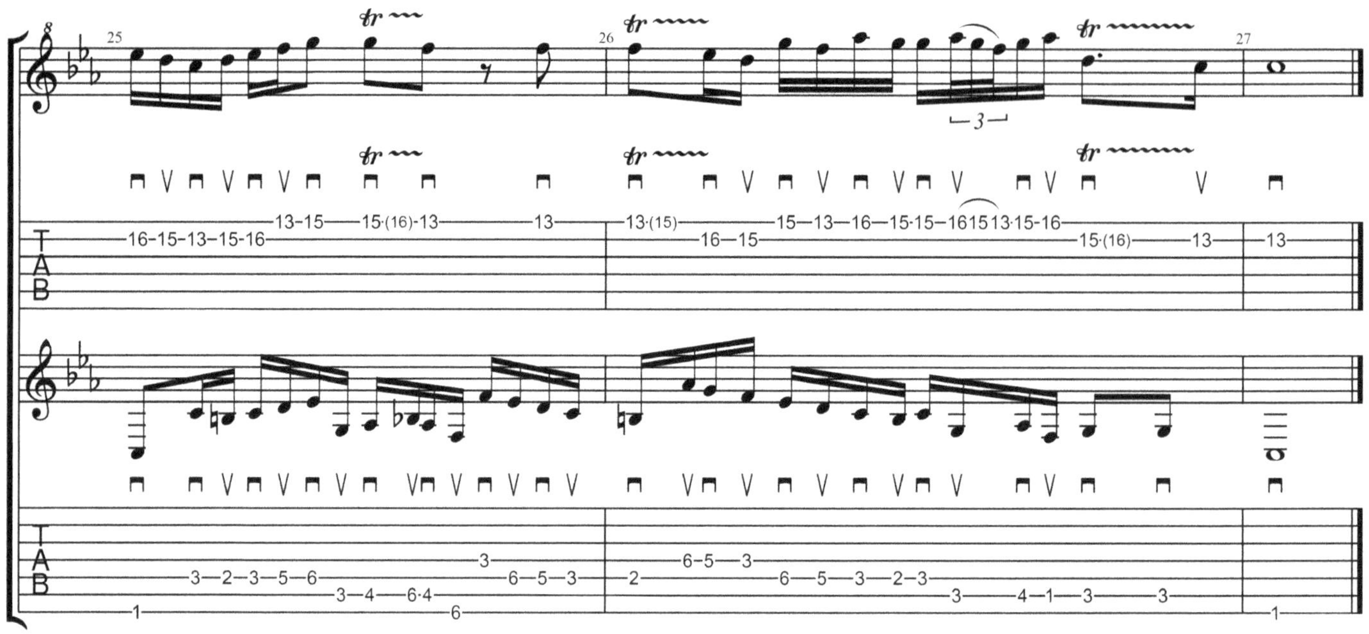
25
26
27
tr
3
T
A
B

Invention Three in D Major

Our third Invention takes us outside the more familiar 4/4 feel and into the less common 3/8 time signature.

In a time signature, the first number tells us how many beats are in each bar, and the second tells us the division of the beat. So 3/8 tells us that there are three 1/8th notes in a bar.

This means we need to count through the piece as *1* 2 3, *1* 2 3, *1* 2 3, *1* 2 3 with accents on the ones.

You could argue that this feels similar to 3/4, and I wouldn't disagree. These days, it would be quite common to write this piece in 3/4, but Bach used 3/8 to suggest a quicker tempo than the more dance-like feel you'd expect from 3/4 time.

In 3/4 time, the music feels like it has three full beats in each bar, with each beat carrying its own weight and space. This gives the rhythm a steady, flowing quality where every beat is clearly defined. By contrast, 3/8 time feels more like one main beat divided into three quicker notes. The result is a lighter, more agile feel, where the bar moves by more quickly and the focus shifts to the overall pulse rather than each individual beat.

Although this piece is in D Major, my favourite phrase occurs in bar eighteen, where we briefly shift to B Minor. The line is built from the B Harmonic Minor scale, where the pattern descends a scale tone, leaps up a third, and then descends four scale tones.

Example 7a:

For fun, let's play that sequence in C Major, and move it down onto the lower strings to see how it can be adapted to a different setting.

Example 7b:

Now let's tackle the full invention

Example 7c:

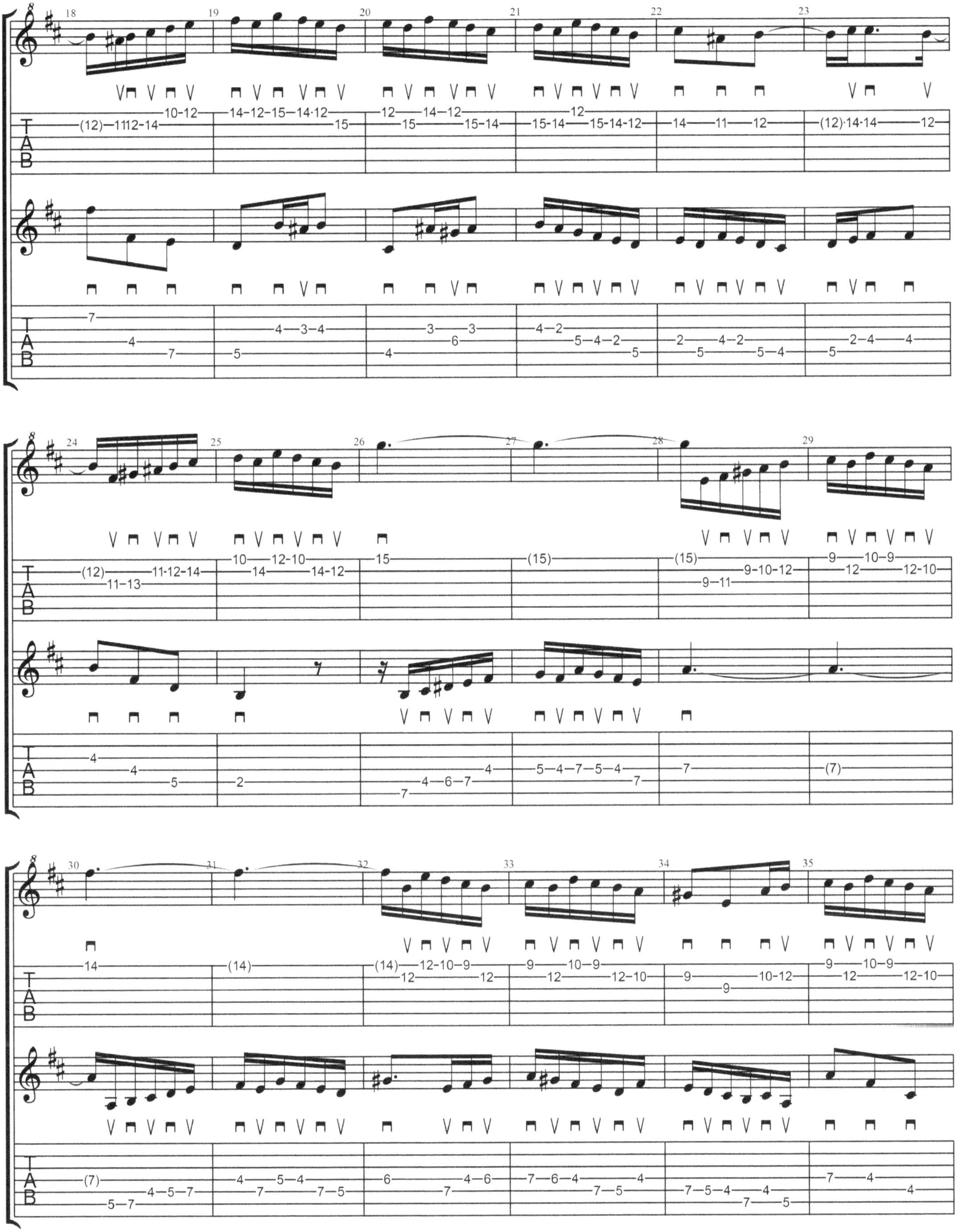

36

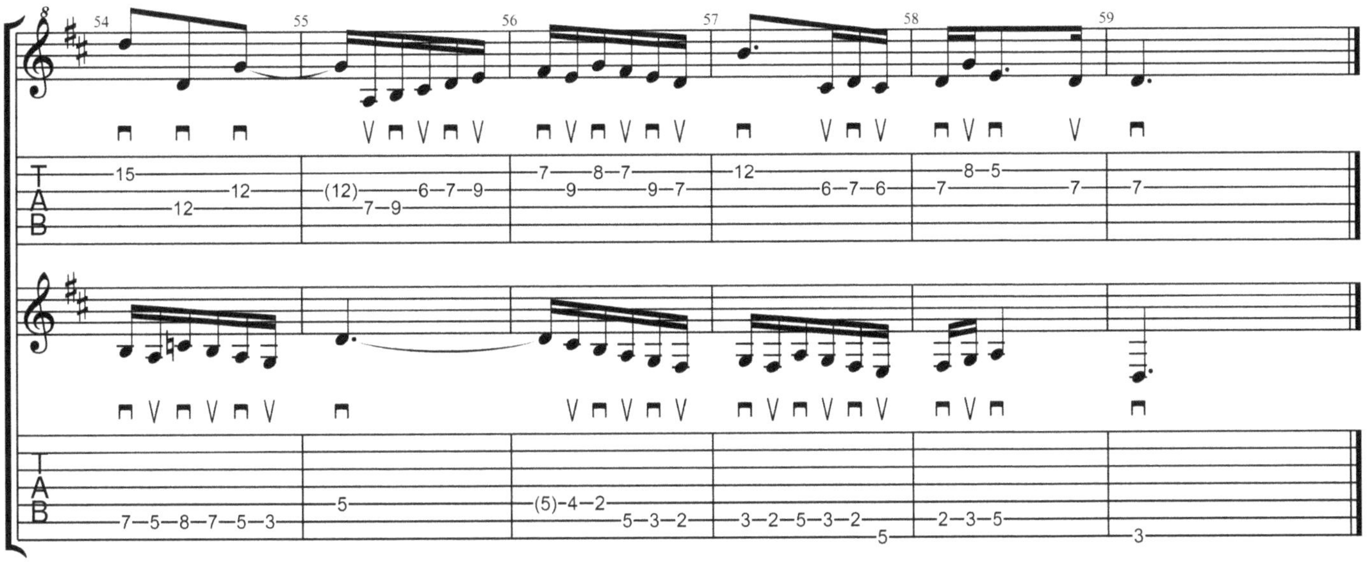
54
55
56
57
58
59
T
A
B
T
A
B

Invention Four in D Minor

The fourth Invention is in D Minor and stays in 3/8 time.

I've approached this piece as a study of Bach's incredible ability to outline harmony with counterpoint. While the original scores don't include chord symbols, it's useful to analyse the lines and add chord symbols throughout the arrangement for your own education.

To do this, we need to look at the sum of what both voices create by combining the notes from scales and arpeggios to reveal the underlying harmony.

A good starting point is to look at the notes that fall on the beats and see if they spell out a familiar chord. In the first few bars, you'll notice that we move between D minor and A Major — the i and V chords in the key of D Minor.

You could also view the second bar as outlining an A7 chord, since it contains all four notes: A, C#, E, and G.

As the piece unfolds, there's a lovely sequence that remains in D Minor and ascends in fourths from one bar to the next. It's quite easy to spot if you look at the role each voice is playing. In each bar, the bass outlines the root of the chord, while the melody sits on the third.

Look at the following to see exactly how it works:

- G bass note and Bb melody = G Minor

- C bass and E melody = C Major

- F bass and A melody = F Major

G Minor	C Major	F Major	Bb Major	Em7b5
iv	bVII	bIII	bVI	ii

This idea gives us a glimpse into the kind of organisation that is happening in Bach's music.

Here's the Invention played in its entirety.

Example 8a:

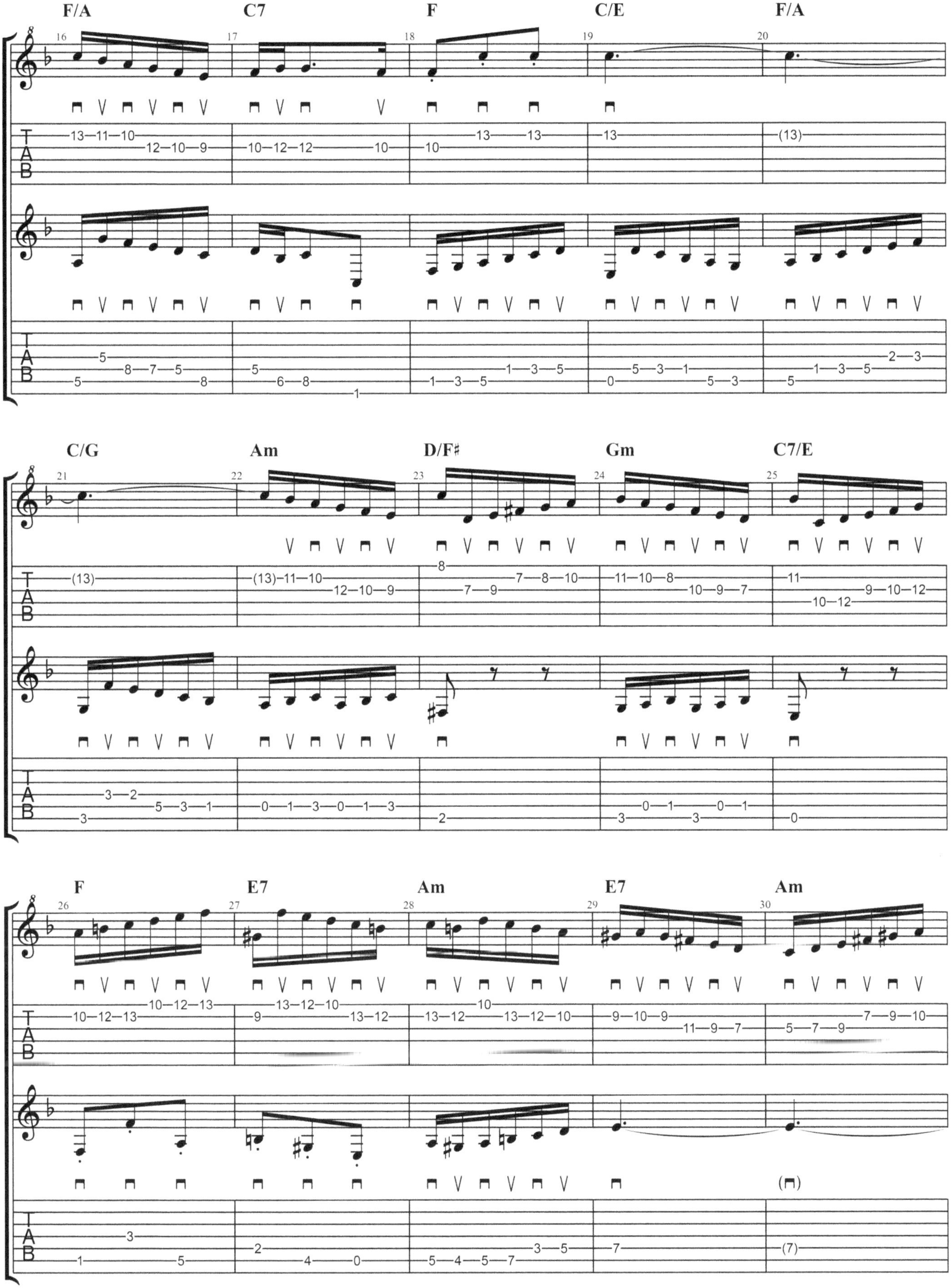
F/A C7 F C/E F/A
C/G Am D/F♯ Gm C7/E
F E7 Am E7 Am

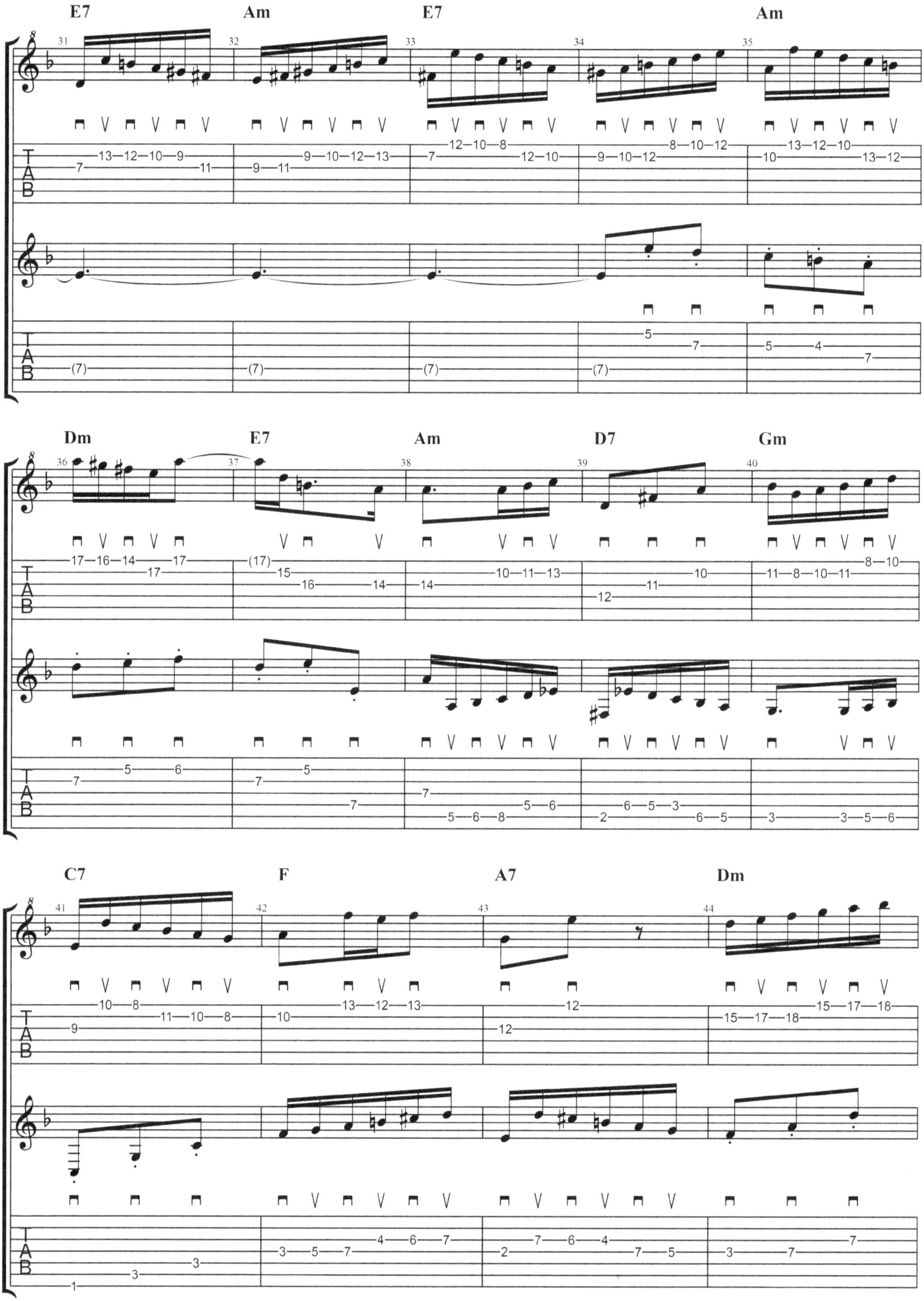
E7
Am
E7
Am
Dm
E7
Am
D7
Gm
C7
F
A7
Dm

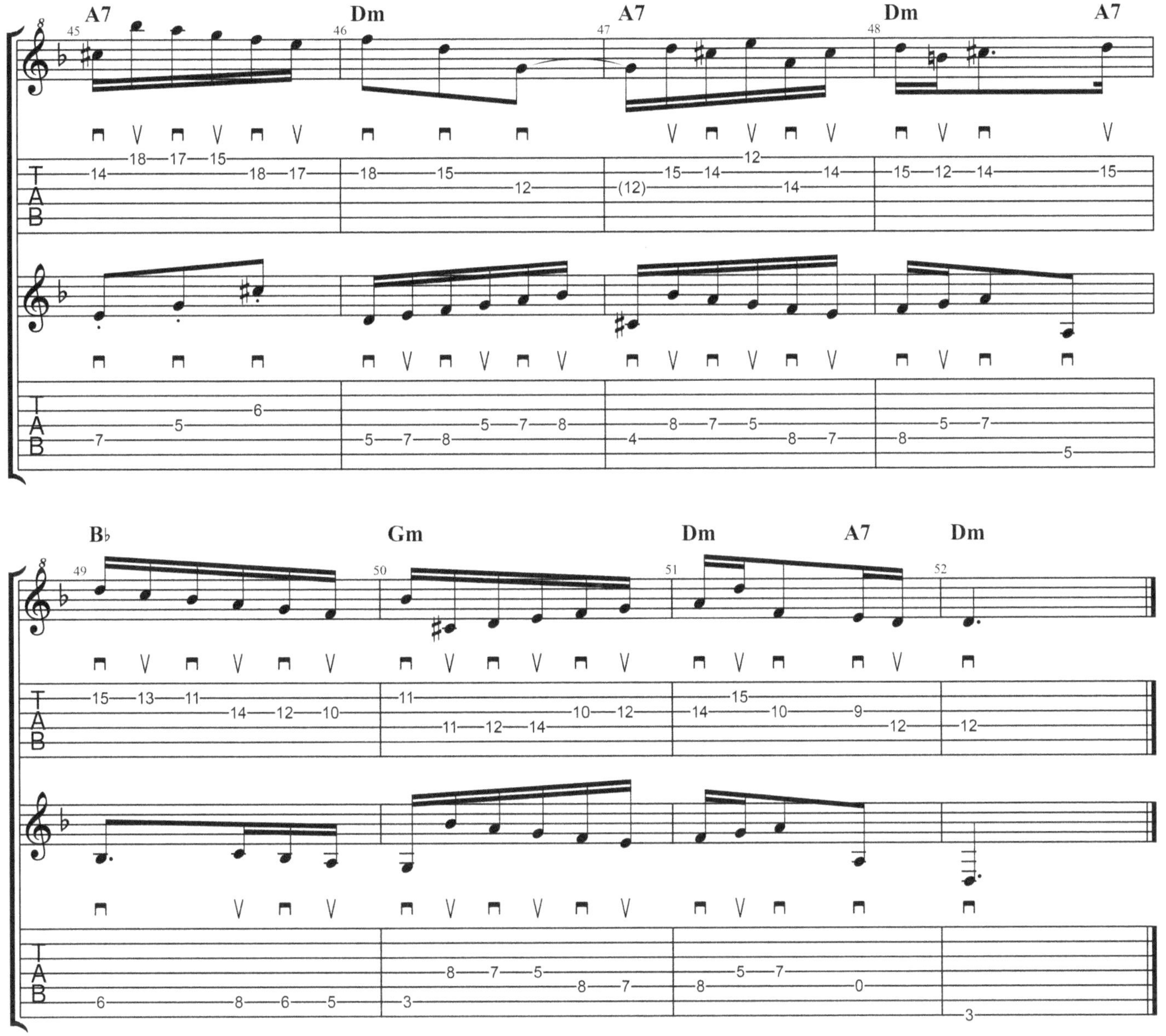
A7
Dm
A7
Dm
A7
B♭
Gm
Dm
A7
Dm

Invention Five in Eb Major

Invention Five takes us back to 4/4 time and into the key of Eb Major.

This one is a real workout, especially for the left hand. There are lots of long, flowing 1/16th note lines paired with pedal tones lower on the neck. You'll need solid finger independence to pull it off, particularly between the ring and pinkie fingers.

It's also a good example of how easily the seven-string arrangements can be adapted for six-string guitar. Here, there are only two notes that appear on the low B string – both of which are an Eb – in the first and final bars. If you're on a six-string, you can simply play the same note an octave higher on the 6th fret of the A string without any issues.

Here is one of my favourite sequences in this piece.

Example 9a:

Although we're in Eb Major, by this point we've added an extra flat (Db) which suggests we've moved into Ab Major. But if you listen closely, that distinctive harmonic minor sound gives it away. We're really in F Minor, the relative minor of Ab Major.

I really enjoy how each new bar features an ascending seventh, followed by a descending fifth at the start of the next bar. These wider interval leaps add shape and movement to the line, keeping things engaging.

Here's a similar idea, this time adapted to a C7 chord on a lower string set.

Example 9b:

Now let's play through the entire Invention.

Example 9c:

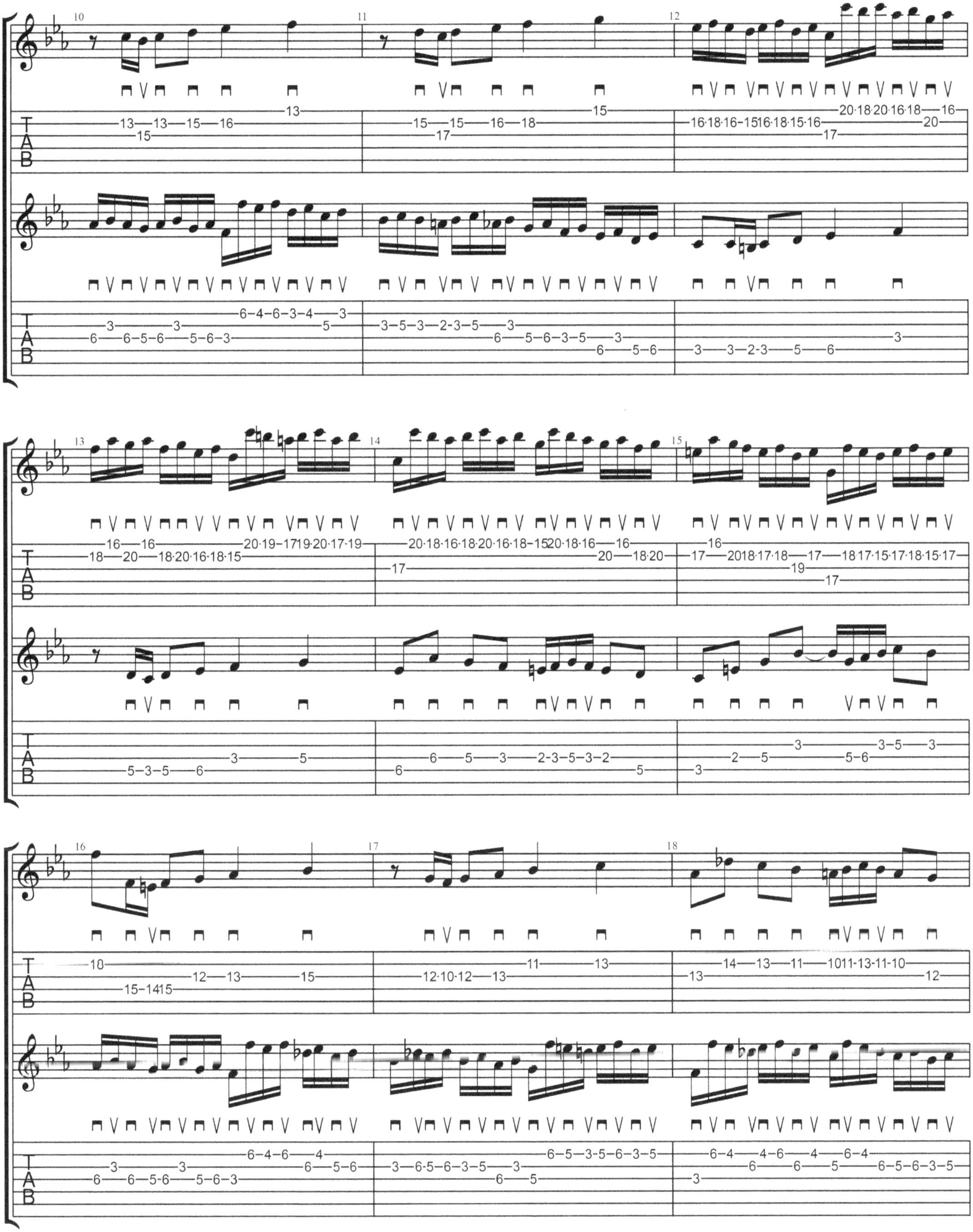

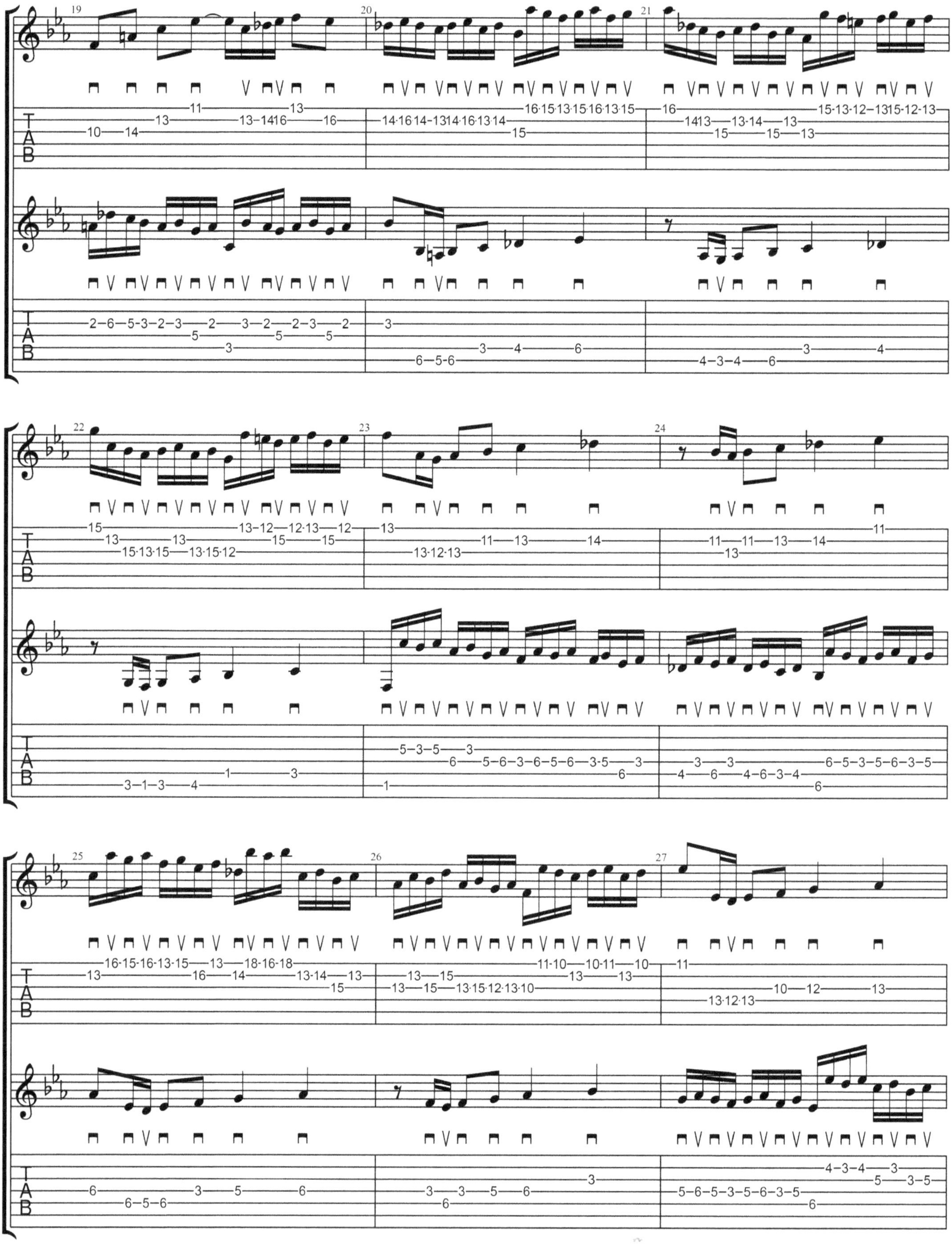

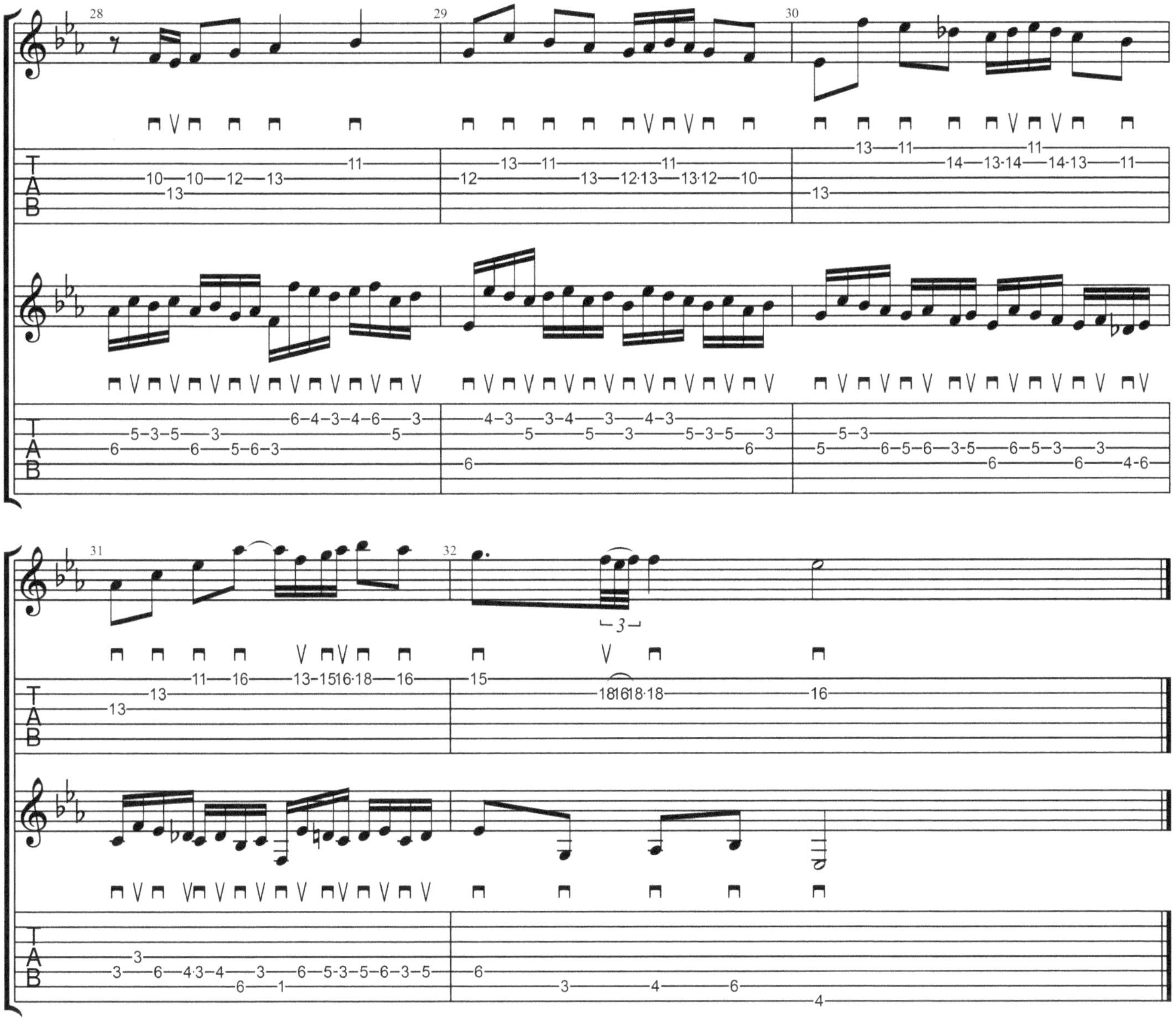
28
29
30
31
32

Invention Six in E Major

Breaking the pattern, we're not moving to Eb Minor here. Instead, we go straight into E Major and return to one of Bach's favourite time signatures of 3/8.

This piece is a wonderful study in syncopation. In this piece, Bach plays with the relationship between the voices by placing the melody off the beat, while the bass keeps the beat, then flipping everything so that the bass takes the off-beat role while the melody locks into the pulse.

In the first few bars, you'll notice the melody is picked entirely with upstrokes, which helps emphasise that the notes are landing off the beat. The melody descends, while the bass moves upward, creating a lovely contrast between the parts.

Example 10a:

Conceptually, this approach is quite straightforward. When you adapt it for a single guitar, you'll find you're simply alternating between a high and low note, with no gaps between them.

To make the string skips more manageable, I'd recommend using your thumb and a finger to play the parts as it helps keep everything clean and controlled.

Example 10b:

When played by one person on the guitar or keyboard, it becomes clear that you're simply alternating between the two voices. However, isolating and playing just the syncopated part takes a bit of control, especially to stay locked into the off-beat feel.

I'd recommend practicing this first using a single note. Alternate between playing on the beat and off the beat until that off-beat placement starts to feel natural.

Keep your picking hand moving the whole time. Focus on the skipped downstroke, then come back up to strike the next note with an upstroke. That steady motion is what keeps everything in time.

Example 10c:

Here's the Invention played in full. It's worth noting that this is the only Invention where Bach includes repeat markings, with both the A and B sections played twice. I've left the repeats out of the recording, simply to avoid giving you a three-and-a-half-minute track to work through.

Example 10d:

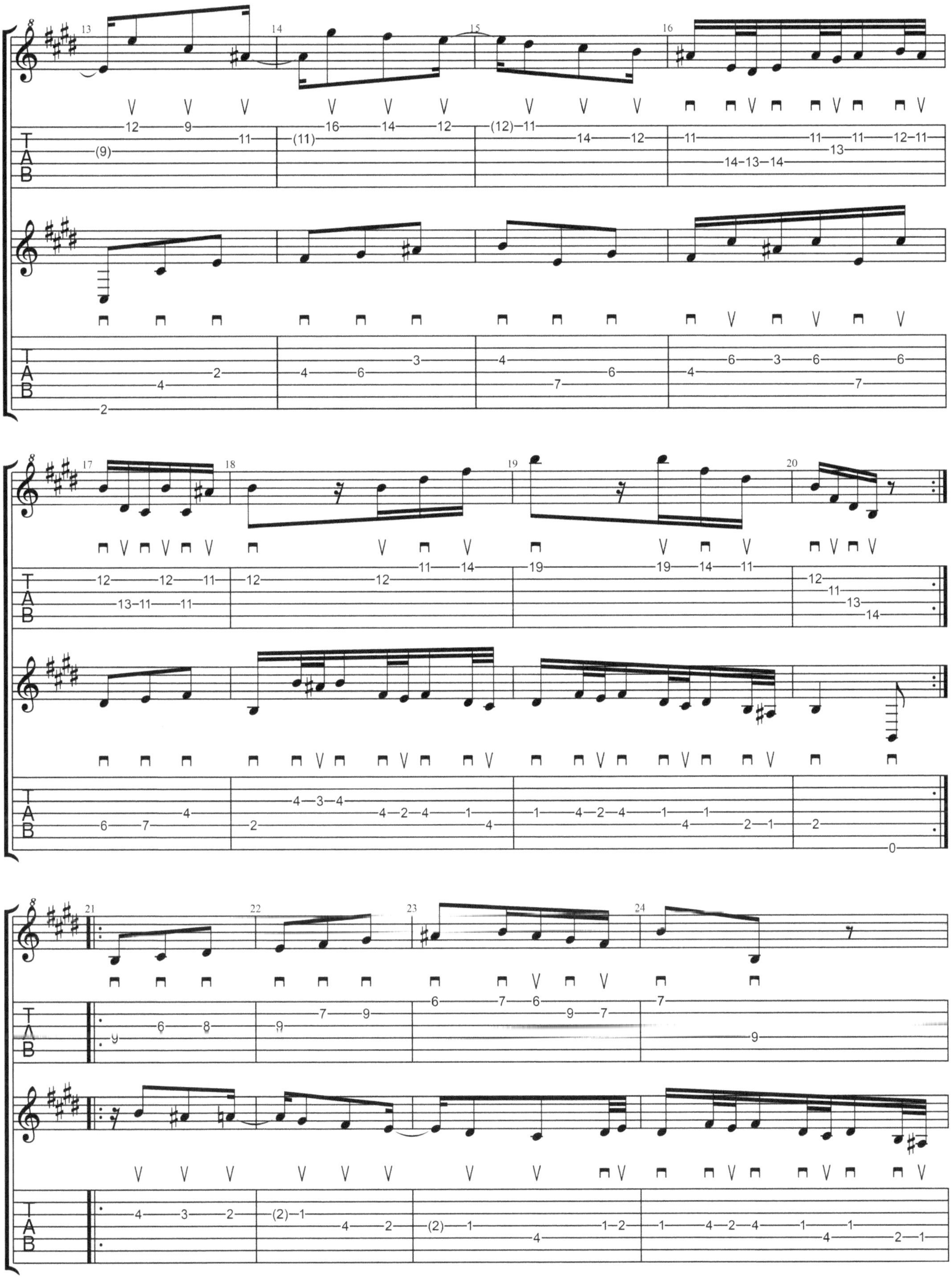

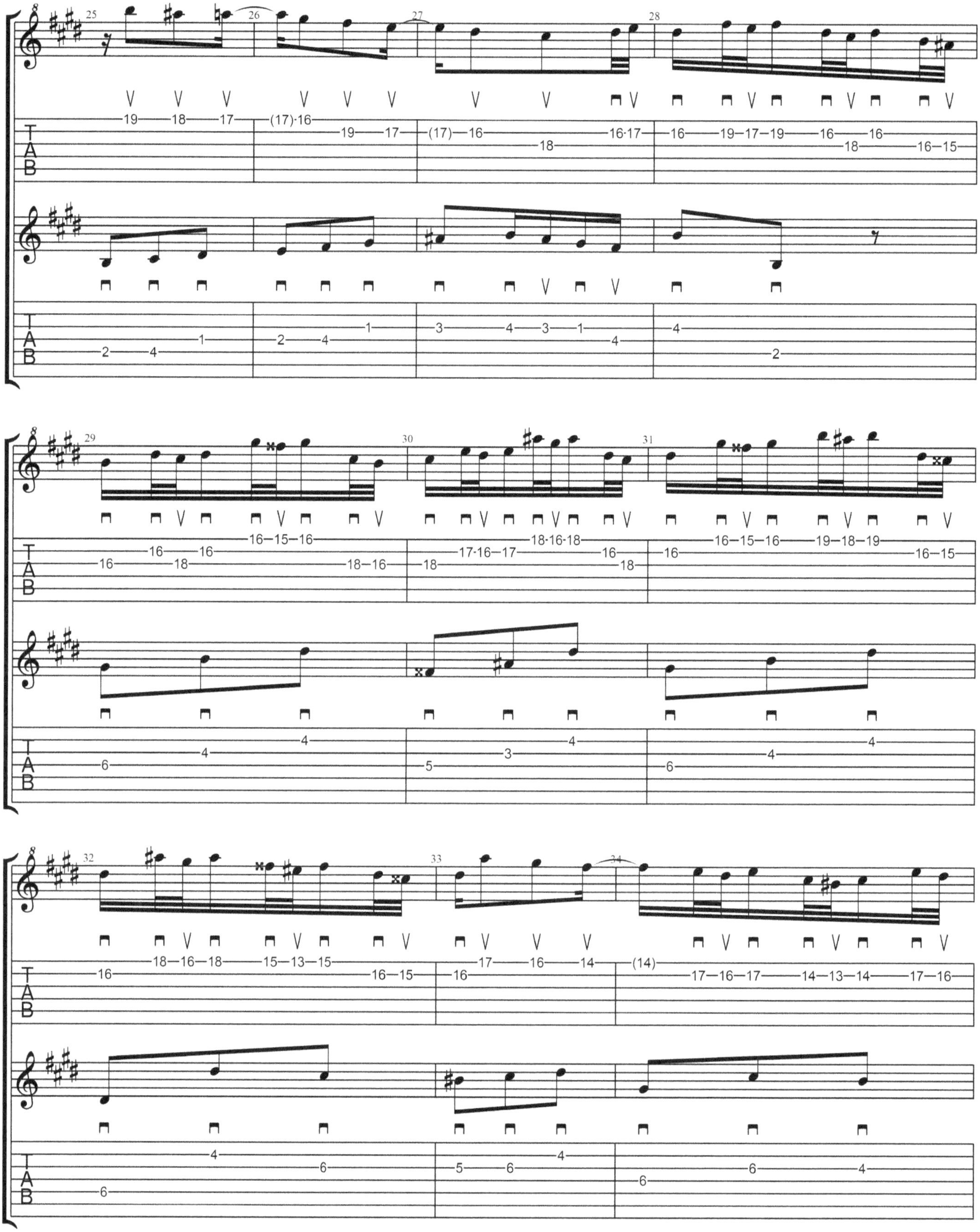

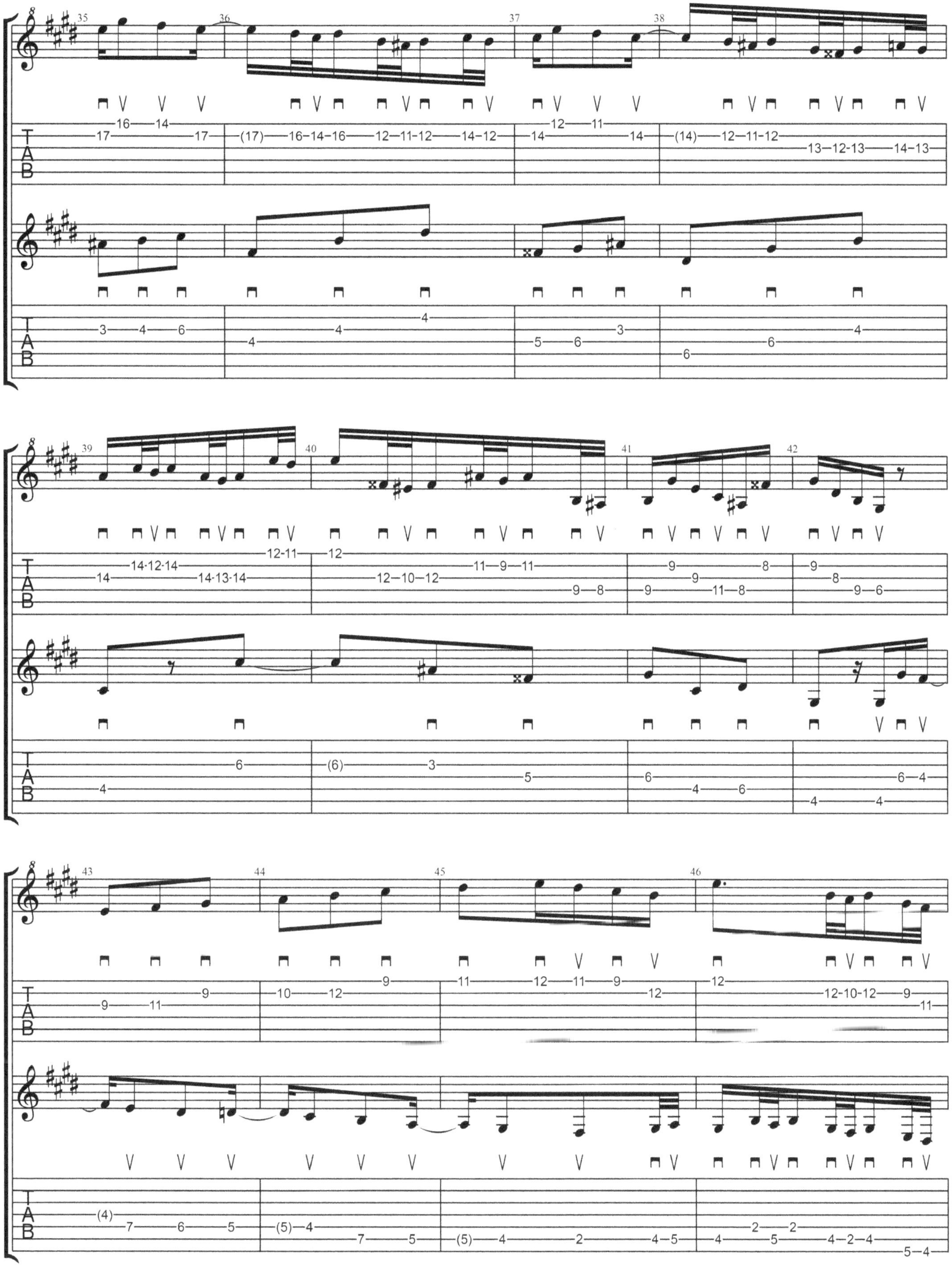

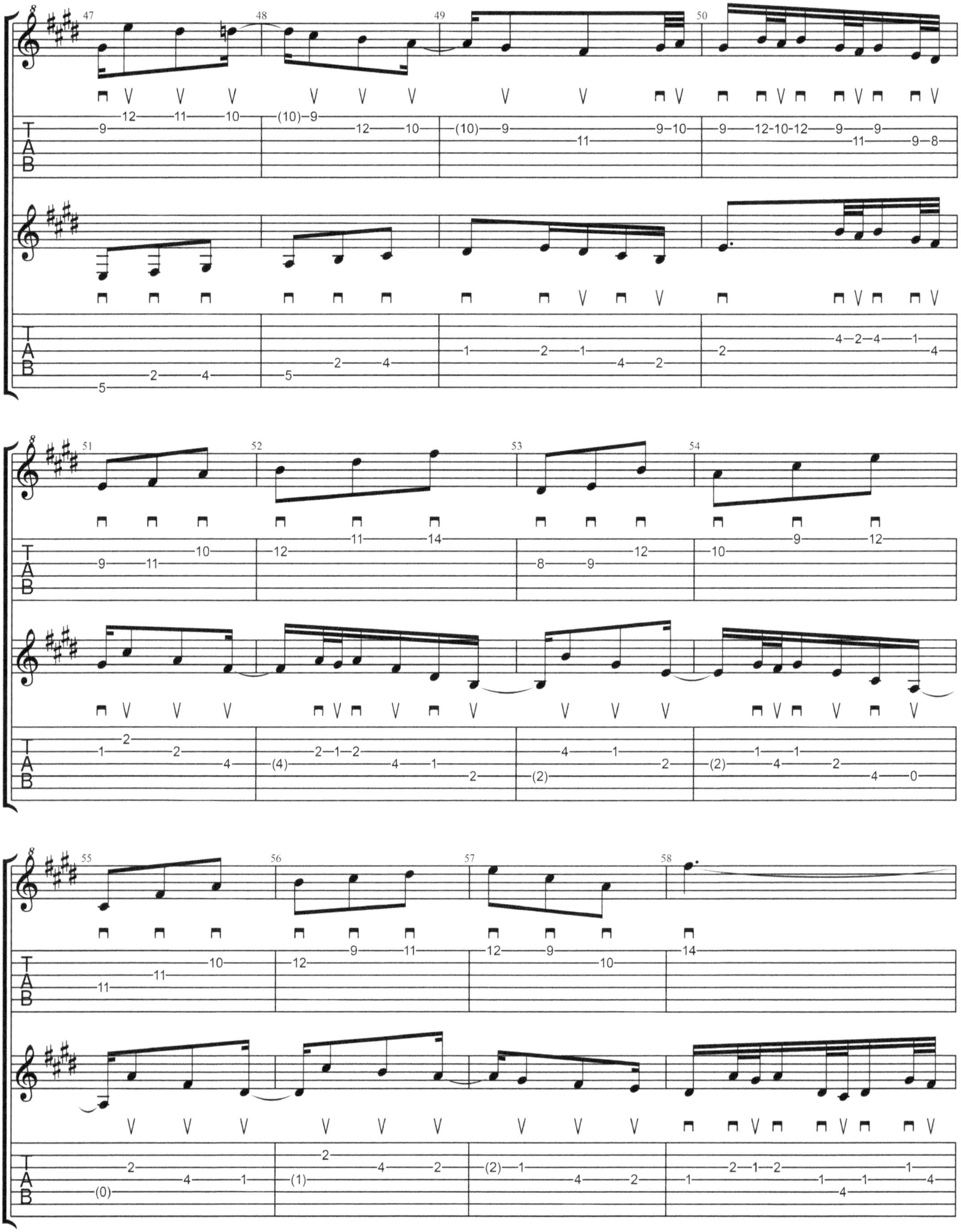

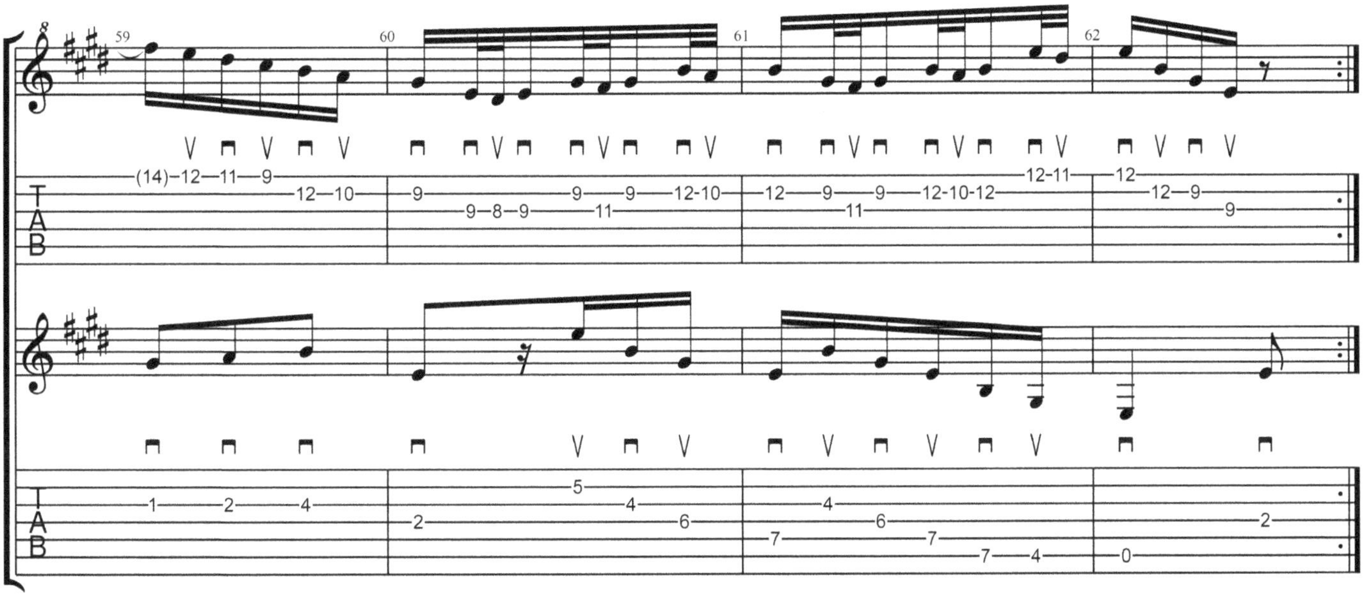
59
60
61
62
TAB
TAB

Invention Seven in E Minor

Now we're in every guitarist's favourite key of E Minor, but blues licks are strictly off the menu!

The tempo here is quite relaxed, which gives you a good opportunity to focus on getting the fingering comfortable, especially when you move up into the 19th and 20th fret area.

As with the other inventions, there are loads of brilliant sequences to explore, but my personal favourite is this elegant idea that blends triads with scale movement. It's a one-note-per-string pattern, which makes it quite demanding to alternate pick cleanly at speed, so keep a close eye on your accuracy as you build it up.

Example 11a:

It gets even more challenging when you shift the idea onto the lower strings and use it to outline different chords. In this example, we move through C Major, G Major, F Major, and then back to C Major, adding a few chromatic notes beneath the ascending arpeggios to keep things interesting.

Example 11b:

Here's Invention Seven played in its entirety.

Example 11c

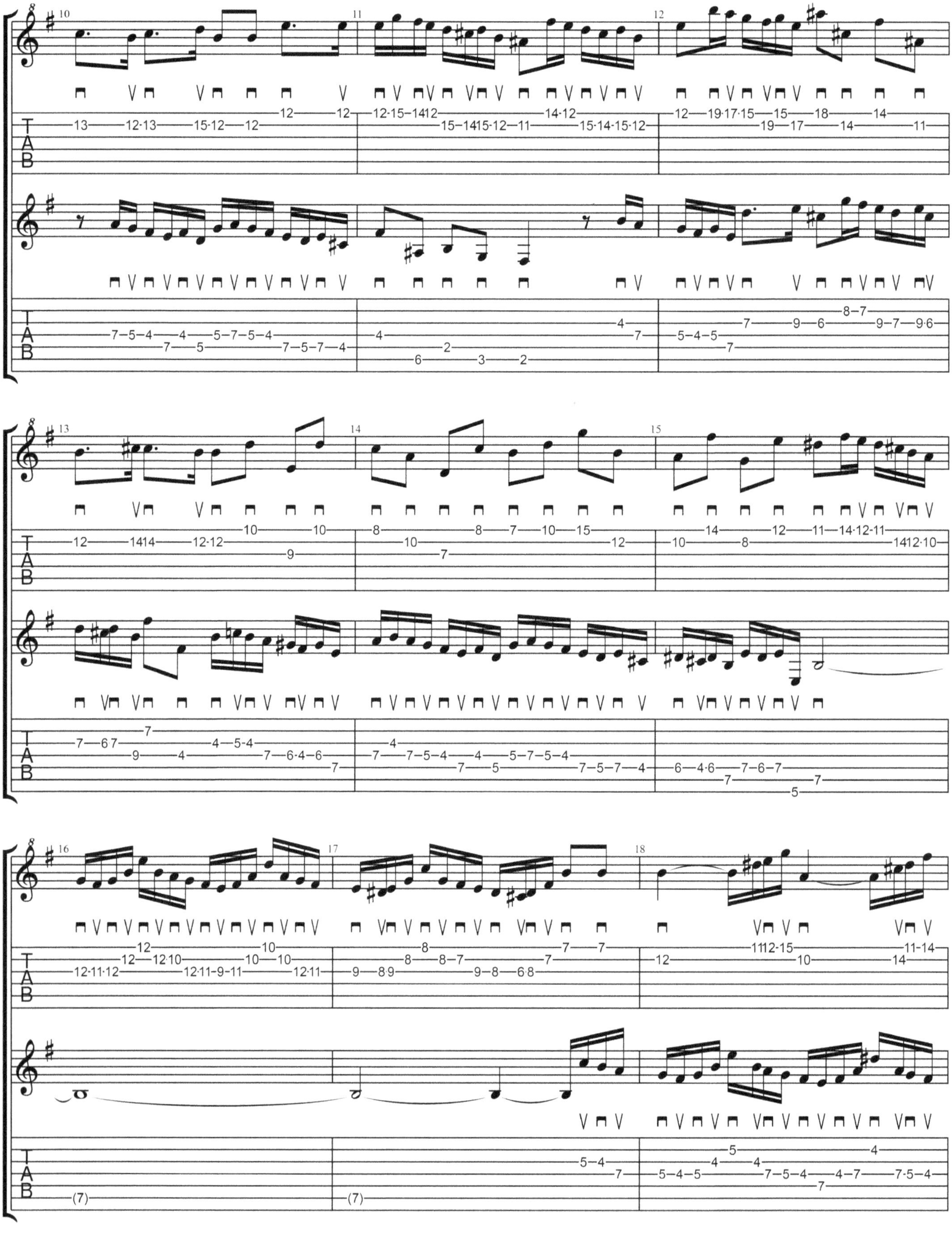

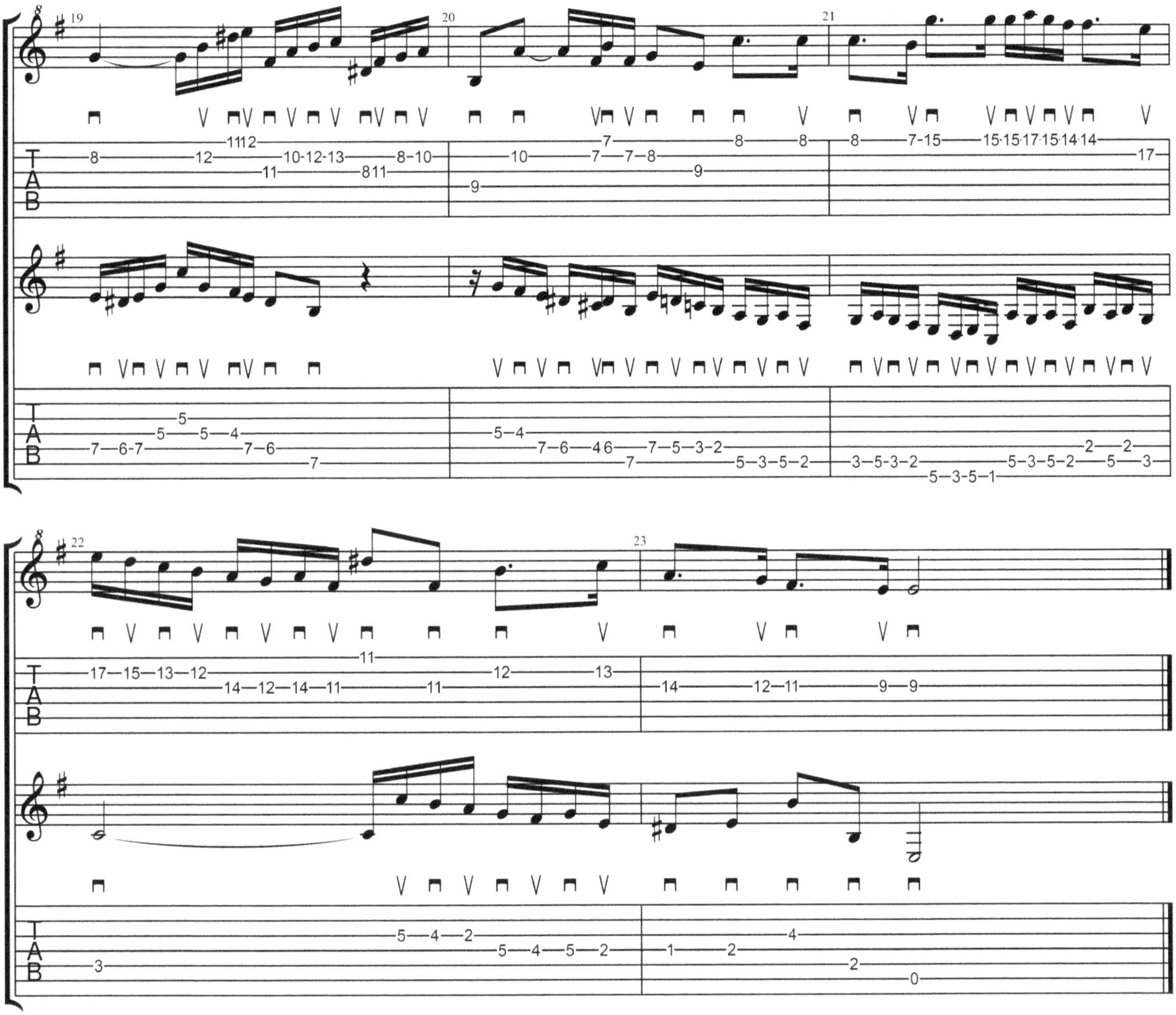

Invention Eight in F Major

This Invention in F Major is one of Bach's best-known pieces from the set and might even be considered the "pop hit" of the collection. It's also a nice reminder that Bach made deliberate choices with time signatures, as after several inventions in 3/8, we are now in 3/4.

This is often played at quite a pace, but I've taken the liberty of slowing it down slightly to make it more approachable and give you time to really enjoy the details.

There are plenty of lovely moments in this piece, but I'd feel like I was keeping something back from you if I didn't highlight the recurring single-string idea. It's a clever pattern where you take three notes on one string, then play the lowest, jump to the highest, drop to the middle, and then return to the highest again.

Example 12a:

This pattern is a favourite among neoclassical players. Some even refer to it as the *I'll See the Light Tonight* pattern – a nod to the solo from the Yngwie Malmsteen shred classic.

The real challenge here lies in keeping your fretting and picking hands perfectly in sync. If they drift even slightly out of time, the whole thing can unravel. Take it slowly to begin with and only build up speed once everything feels solid and controlled.

Example 12b:

There are three fingerings worth spending time on here: index–ring–pinkie, index–middle–pinkie, and the two-tone pattern (which also uses index–middle–pinkie). It's important to be comfortable with all of them, so try not to skip over the one that feels awkward at first.

Now, here's the full Invention.

Example 12c:

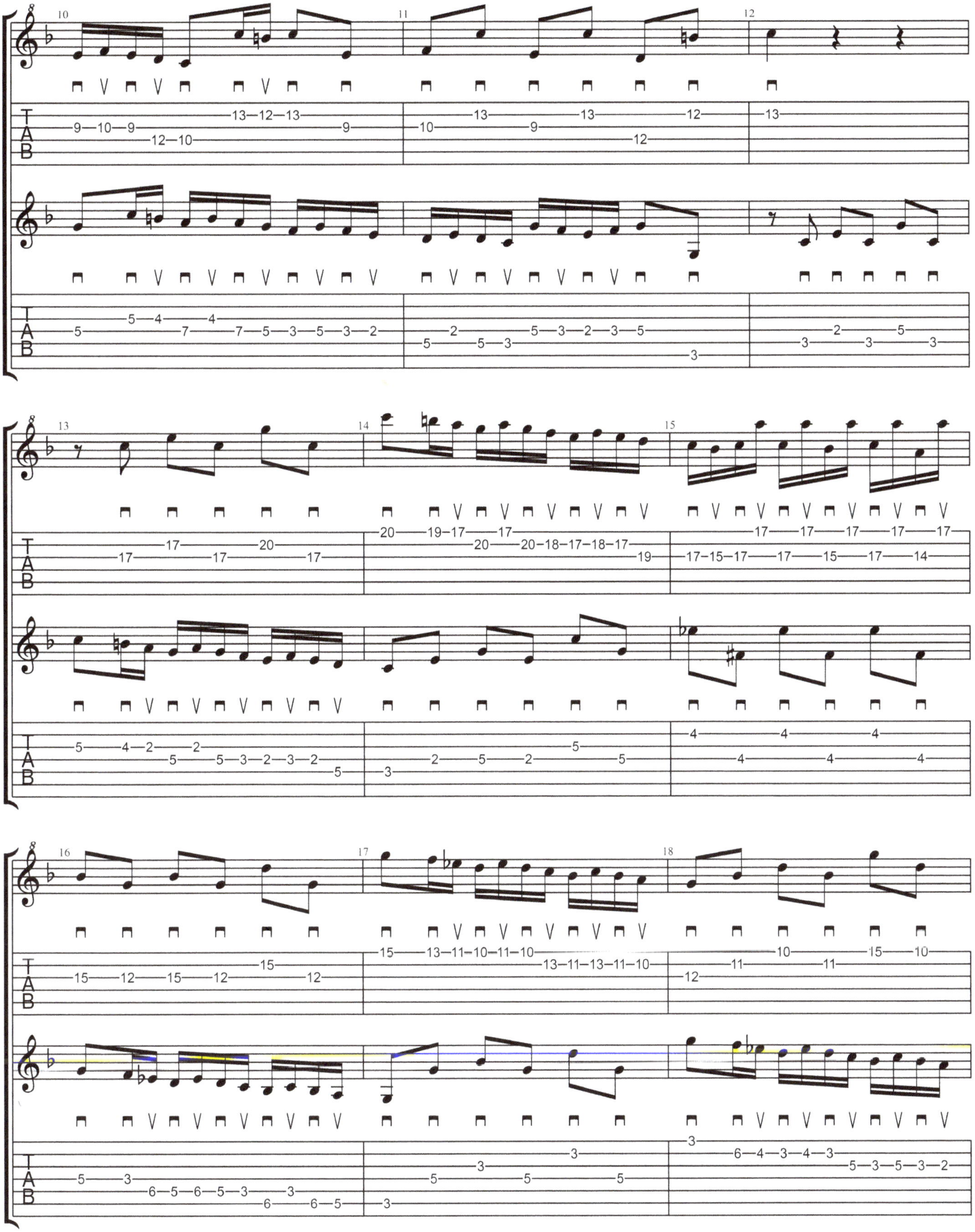
10
11
12
13
14
15
16
17
18
TAB

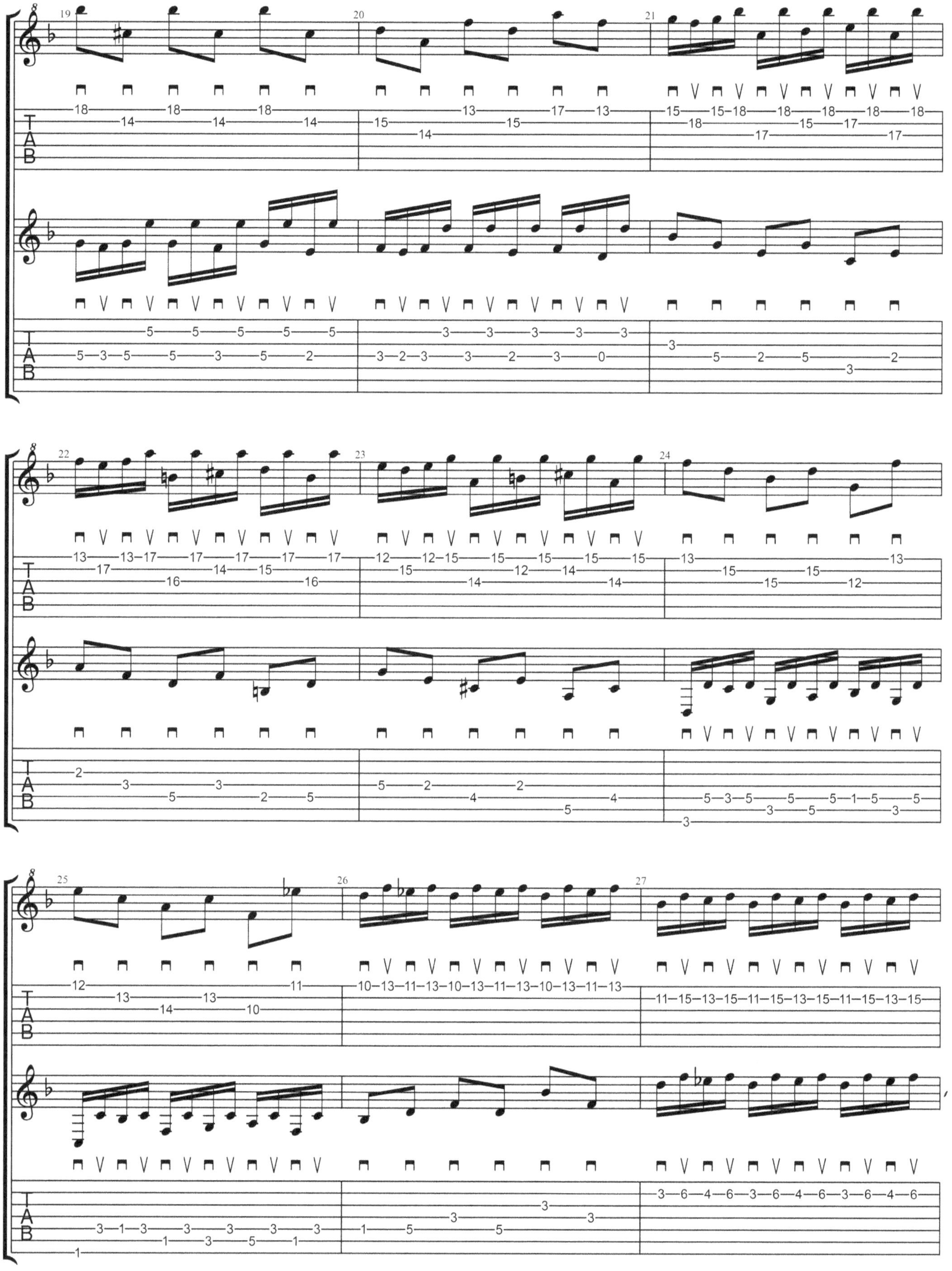

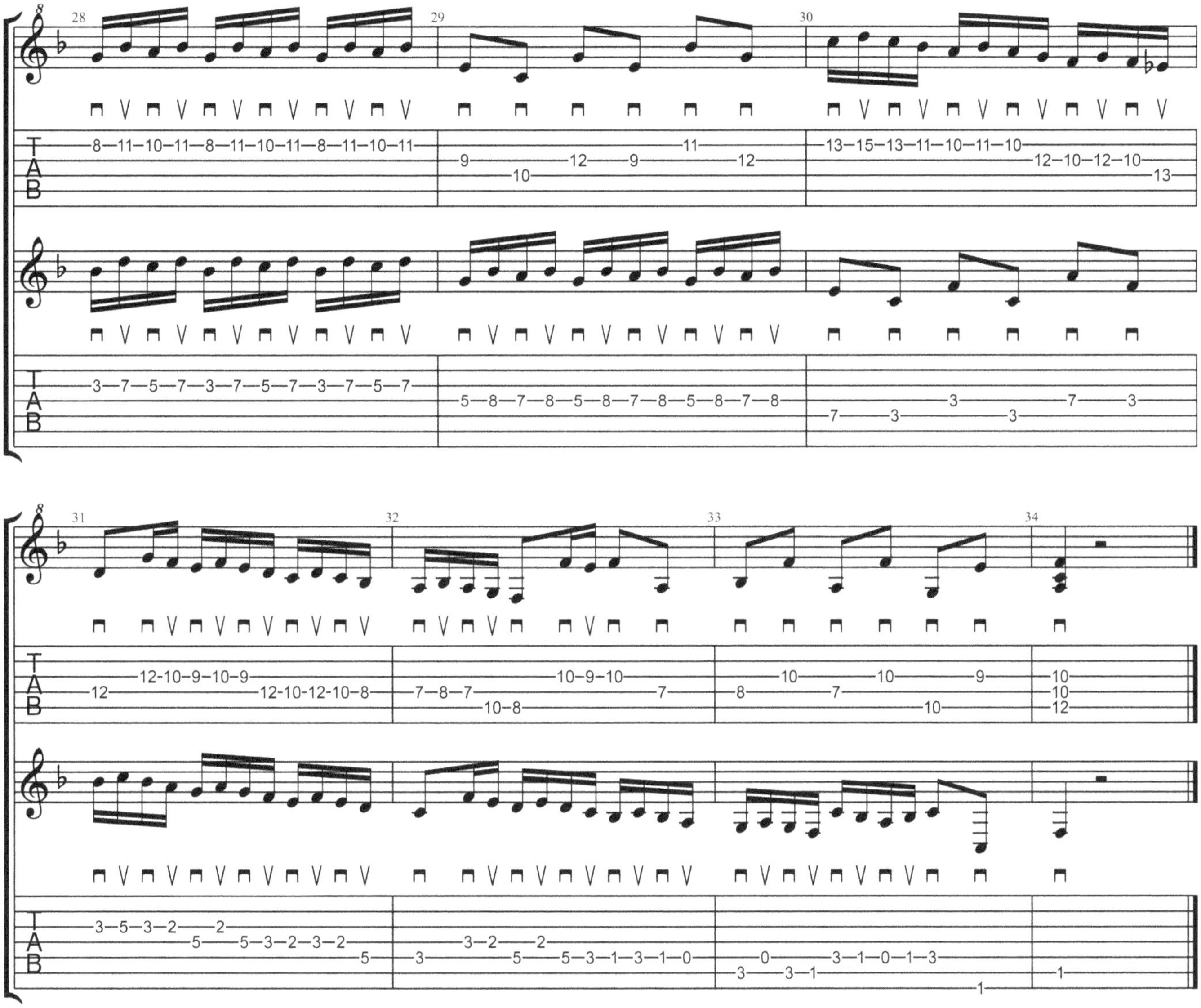

Invention Nine in F Minor

We've talked about some of the technical challenges in these inventions, but never at the expense of melody. Invention Nine could be a great starting point if you're new to this music. It's beautifully melodic, and the slower tempo takes the technical pressure off.

This leads to an interesting question: if nothing here is especially difficult to play, what can we learn from it? (aside from the simple pleasure of playing a piece of music for its own sake!)

Let's examine this section beginning at bar seven and ask ourselves, "What scale is this?"

Example 13a:

The key signature shows F Minor and this key has four flats in the scale: F, G, Ab, Bb, C, Db, Eb, F

However, you'll notice the inclusion of D and E natural notes, which raise both the 6th and 7th degrees of the scale by a semitone (half-step) to create the F Melodic Minor scale: F, G, Ab, Bb, C, D, E, F.

In the classical world, the melodic minor scale is often played when ascending in a minor key, but the natural minor version is played when descending.

Example 13b:

Bach doesn't always stick to this convention though, and you will often find parts where one voice plays the note D natural (from F Melodic Minor) while the other plays Db (from F Natural Minor, and normally occurring in the harmony part). However, the melodic minor sound still comes through clearly.

Here's the full piece.

Example 13c:

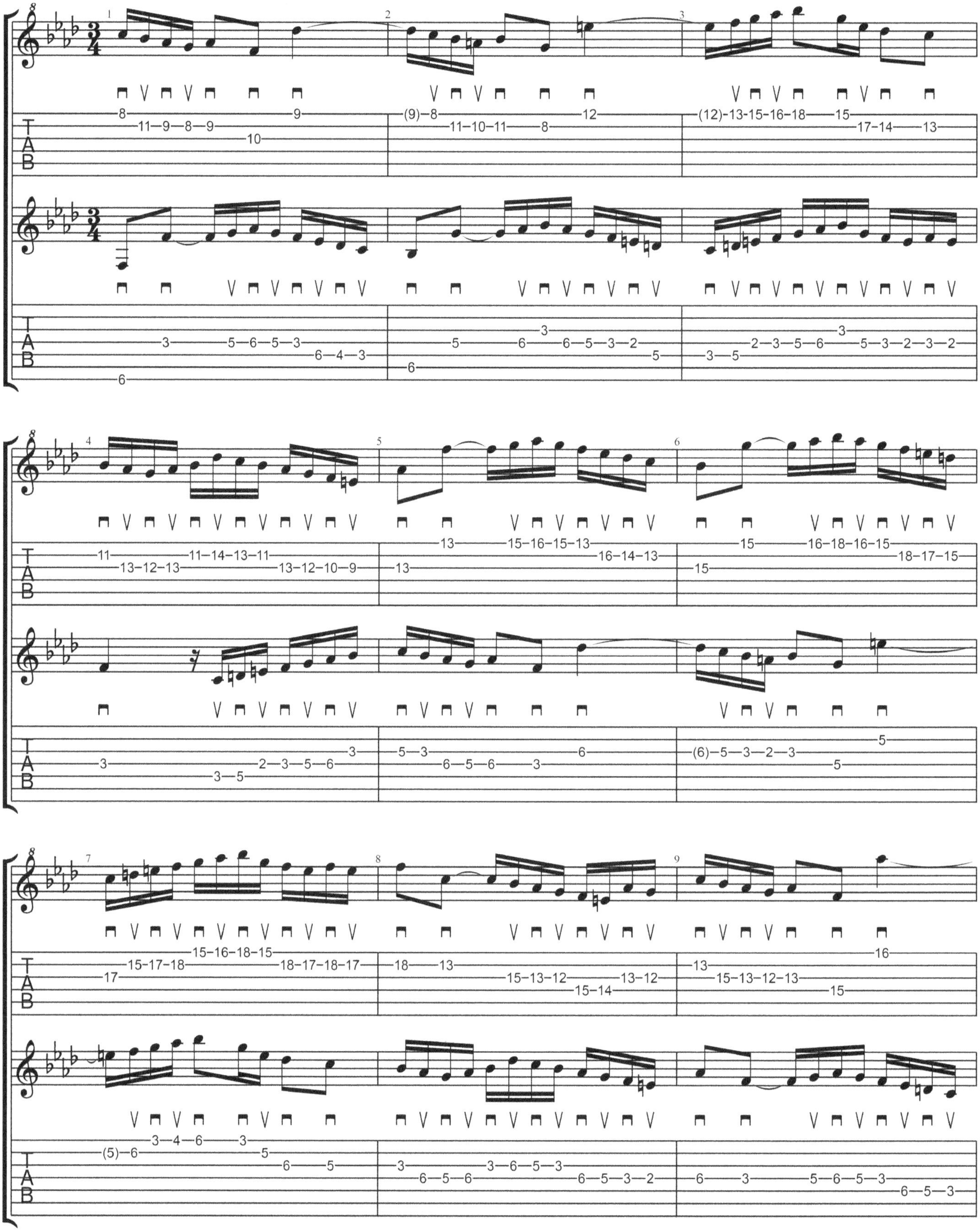

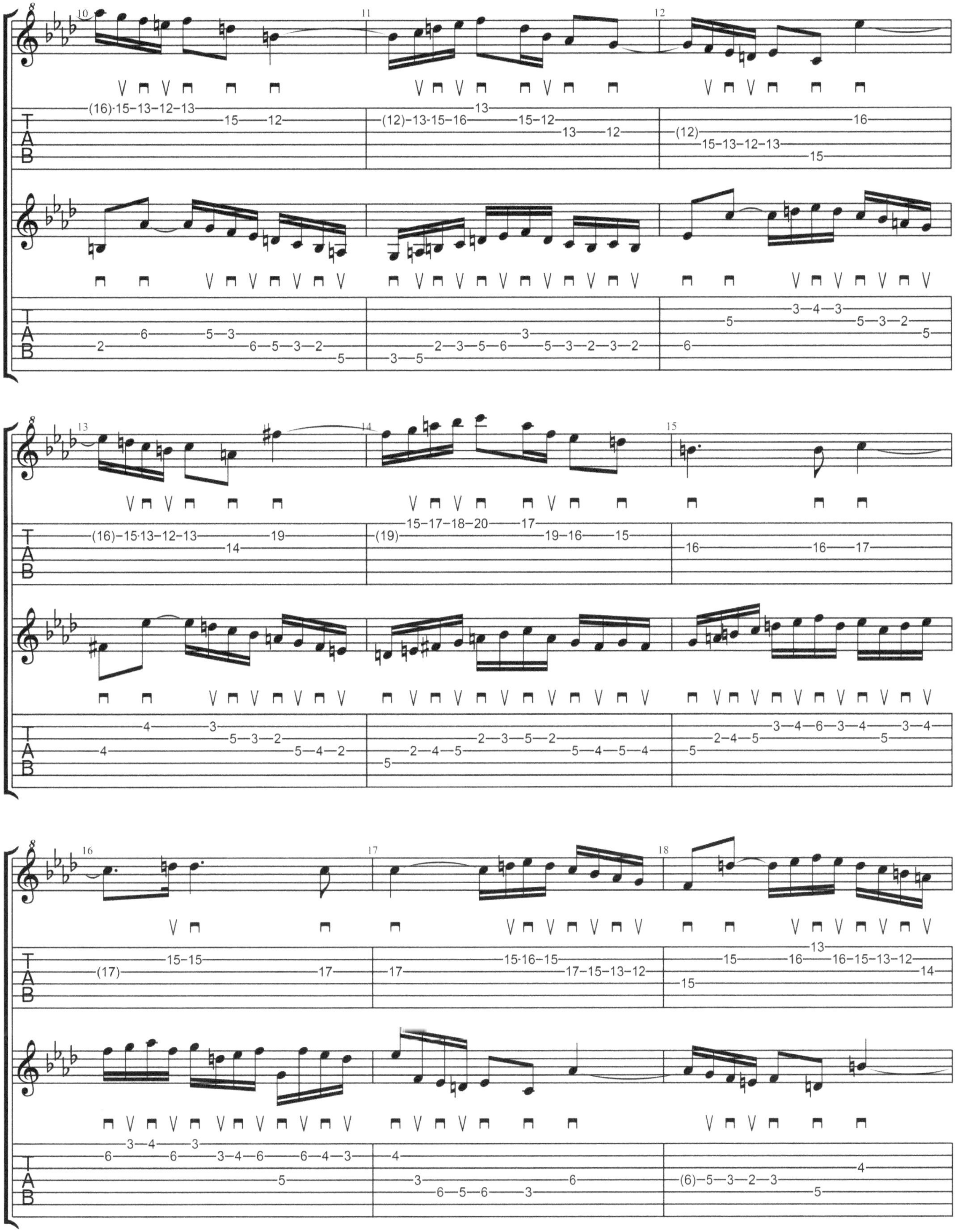

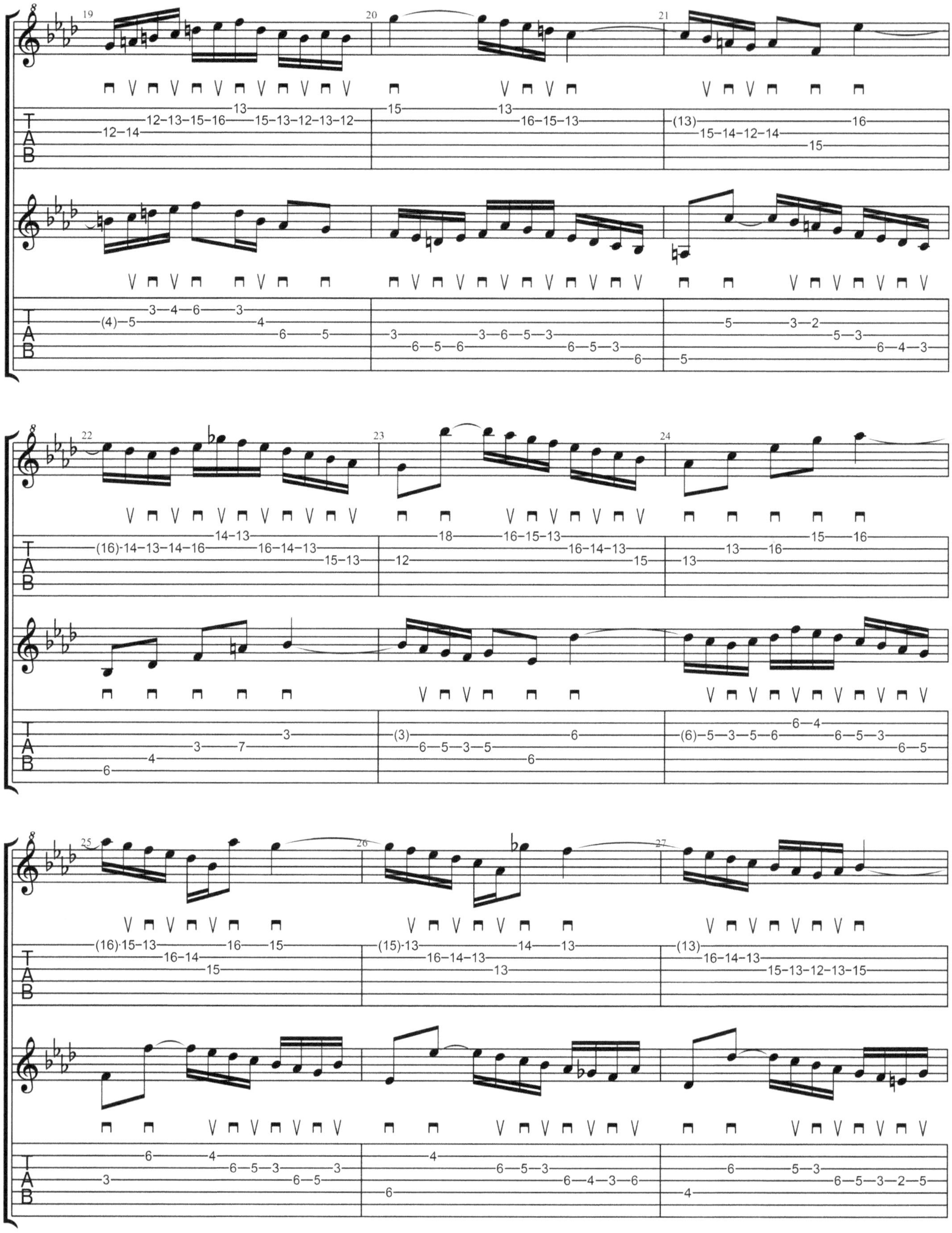

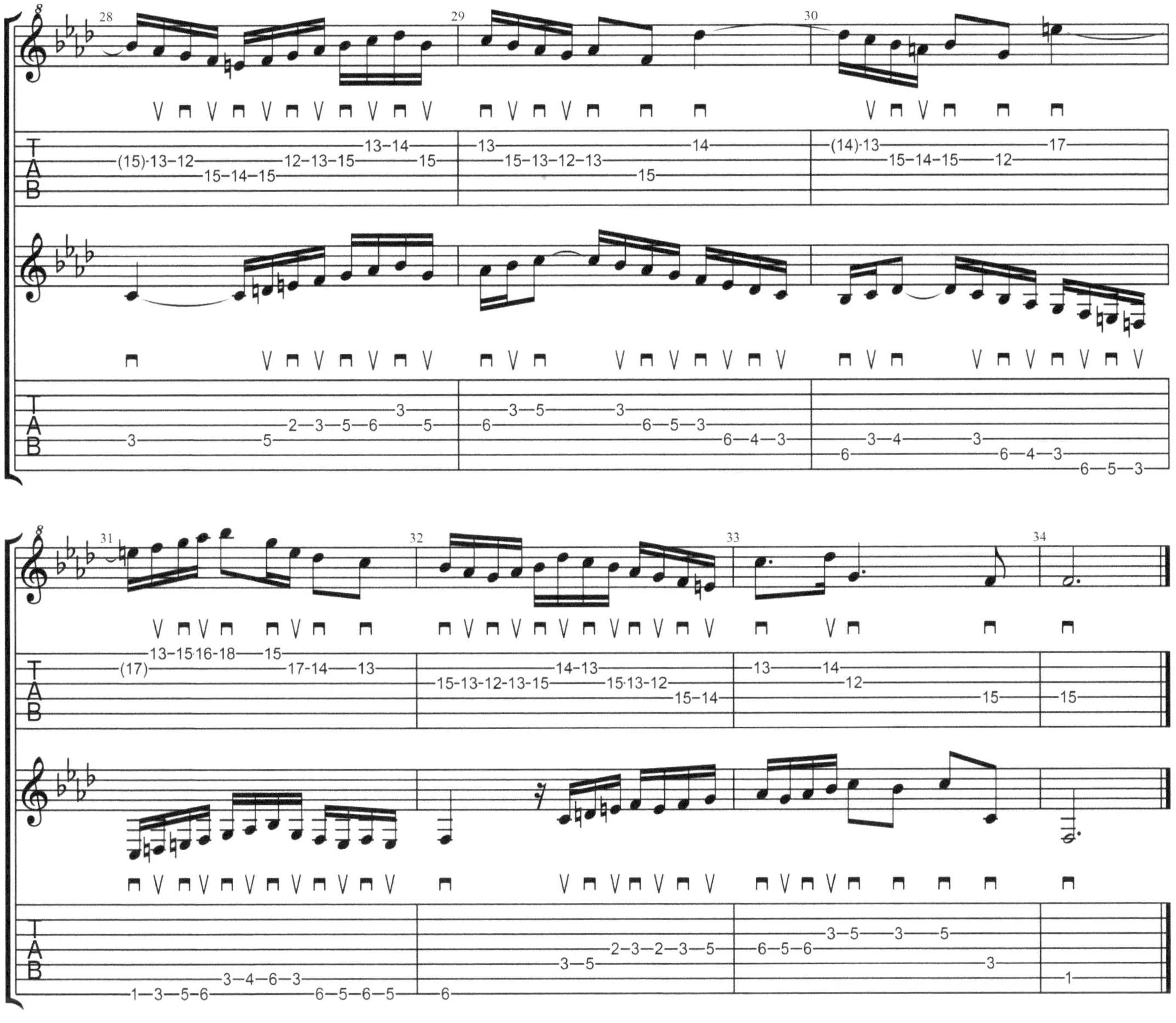

Invention Ten in G Major

Invention Ten is written in 9/8 time which you can think of as 3/4 with each beat divided into a triplet. Writing in 9/8 means we don't need to constantly notate triplet groupings over every set of three notes and keeps the notation looking cleaner

This triplet feel brings a small challenge to the picking hand as beat one starts with a downstroke, but beat two lands on an upstroke. To manage this, I sometimes reset my picking hand during a rest to give me a clean start, although I do try to keep the picking motion as consistent as possible throughout.

One of my favourite parts comes near the end of the piece, where the left-hand part runs through a beautifully written arpeggio sequence. It's a great test of picking control and a rewarding one to get under your fingers.

Example 14a:

To get more from the idea, we can practice it in different positions and octaves. By thinking about each phrase around a chord shape it's not difficult to apply the pattern elsewhere.

Example 14b:

Beyond that, the Invention moves at a steady pace and features plenty of arpeggios, so it's important to stay focused on your string choices and keep everything clean.

Here's Invention Ten in full.

Example 14c:

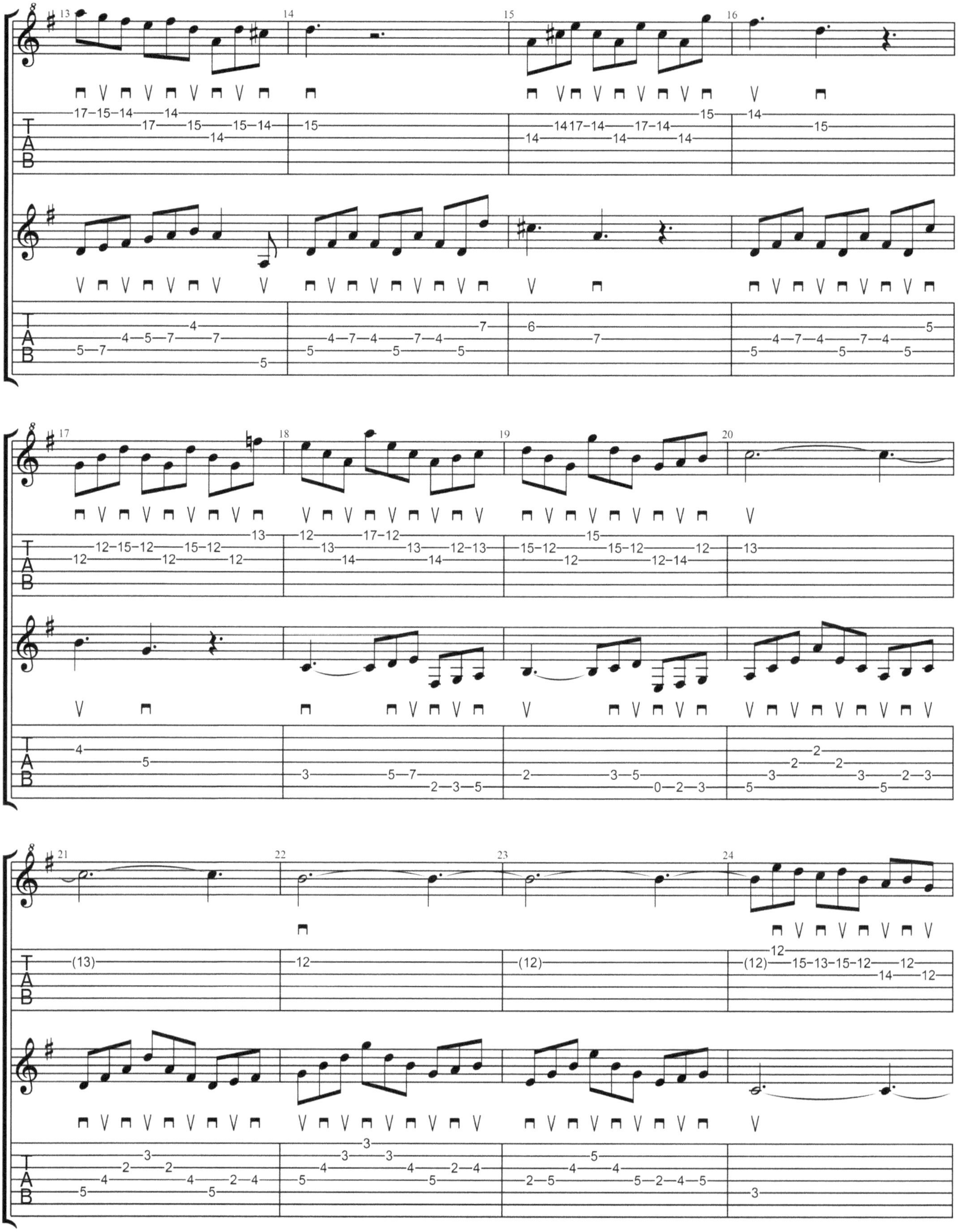

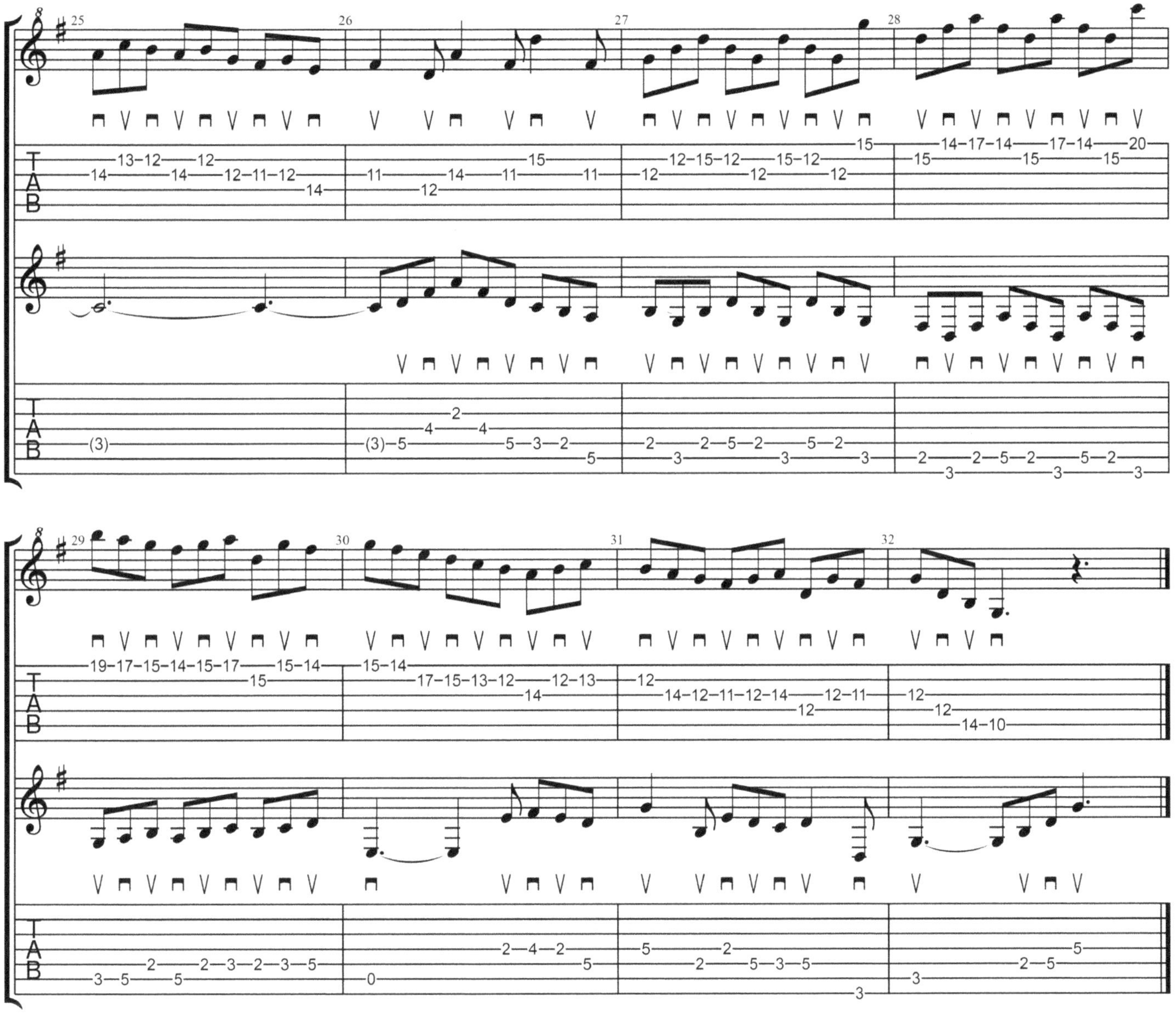

Invention Eleven in G Minor

Invention Eleven returns to 4/4 time and shifts into G Minor. The quicker tempo makes this one a bit more demanding, particularly with the steady flow of 1/16th notes.

One of the standout ideas in this piece is Bach's clever use of chromaticism to link melodic fragments together. It creates smooth transitions and adds a touch of tension that keeps the line moving forward.

Example 15a:

We can adapt this approach to link any two scale positions.

Example 15b:

You'll also hear a similar idea in the left hand, this time in a descending pattern.

Example 15c:

Let's bring that all together in the full version.

Example 15d:

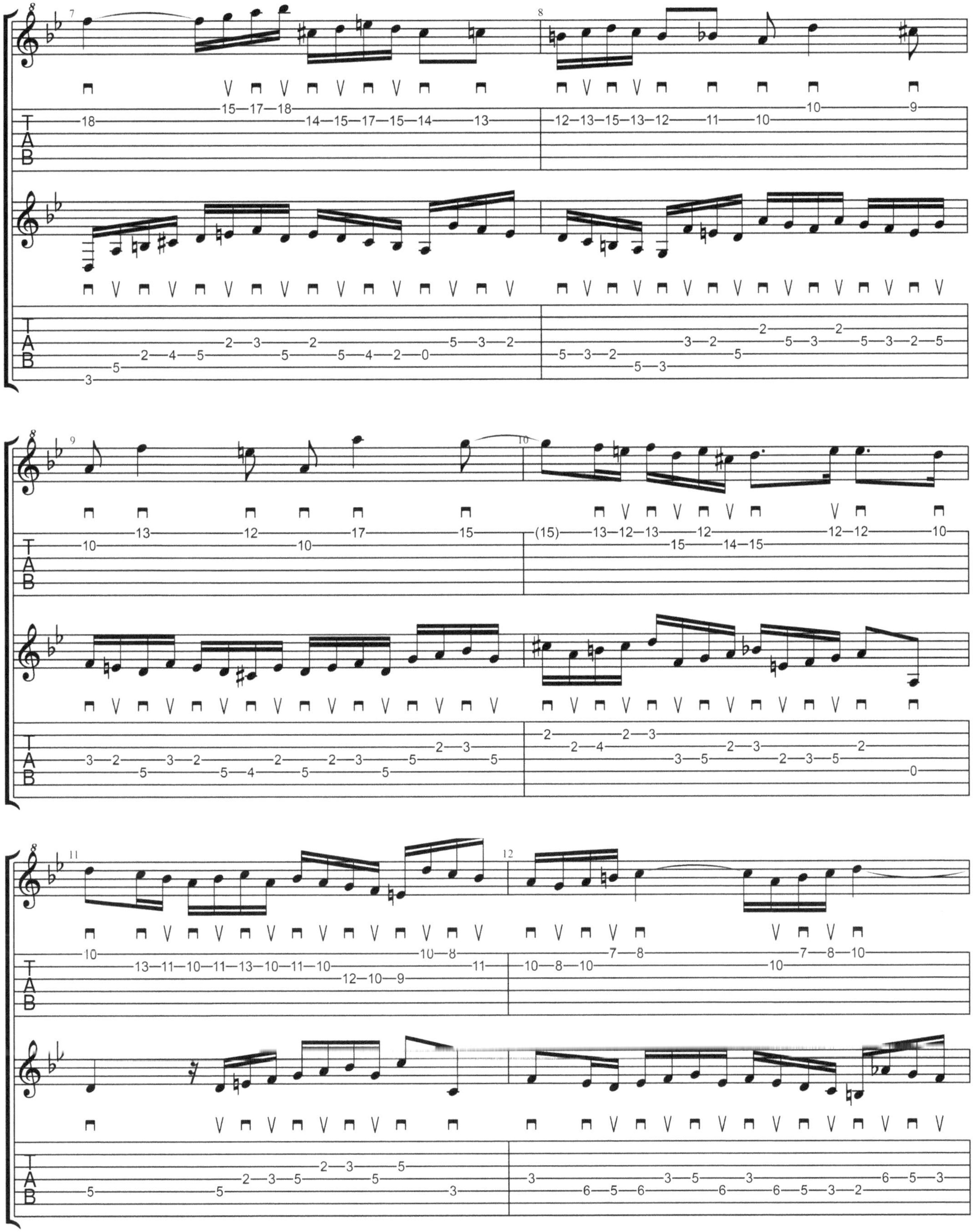

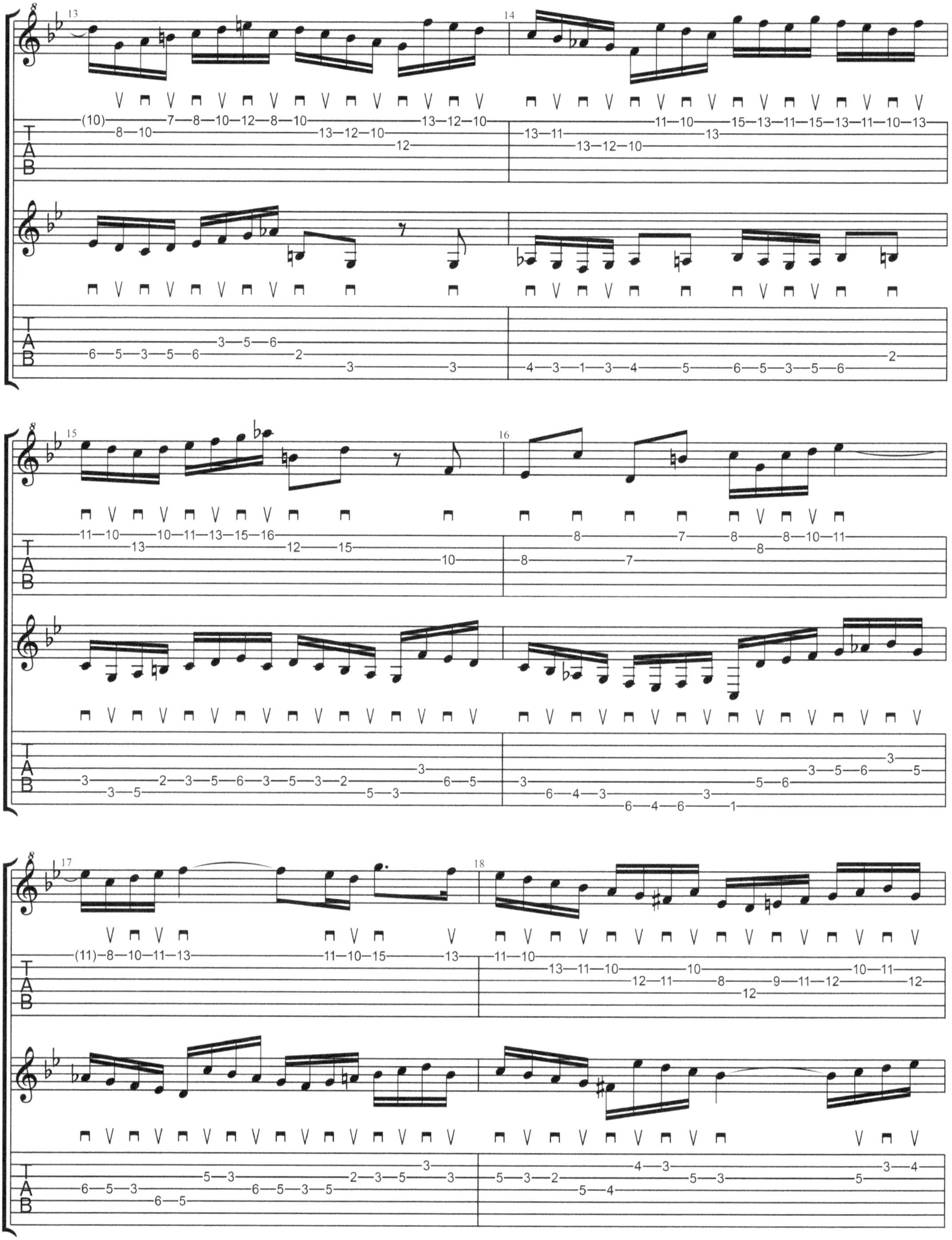

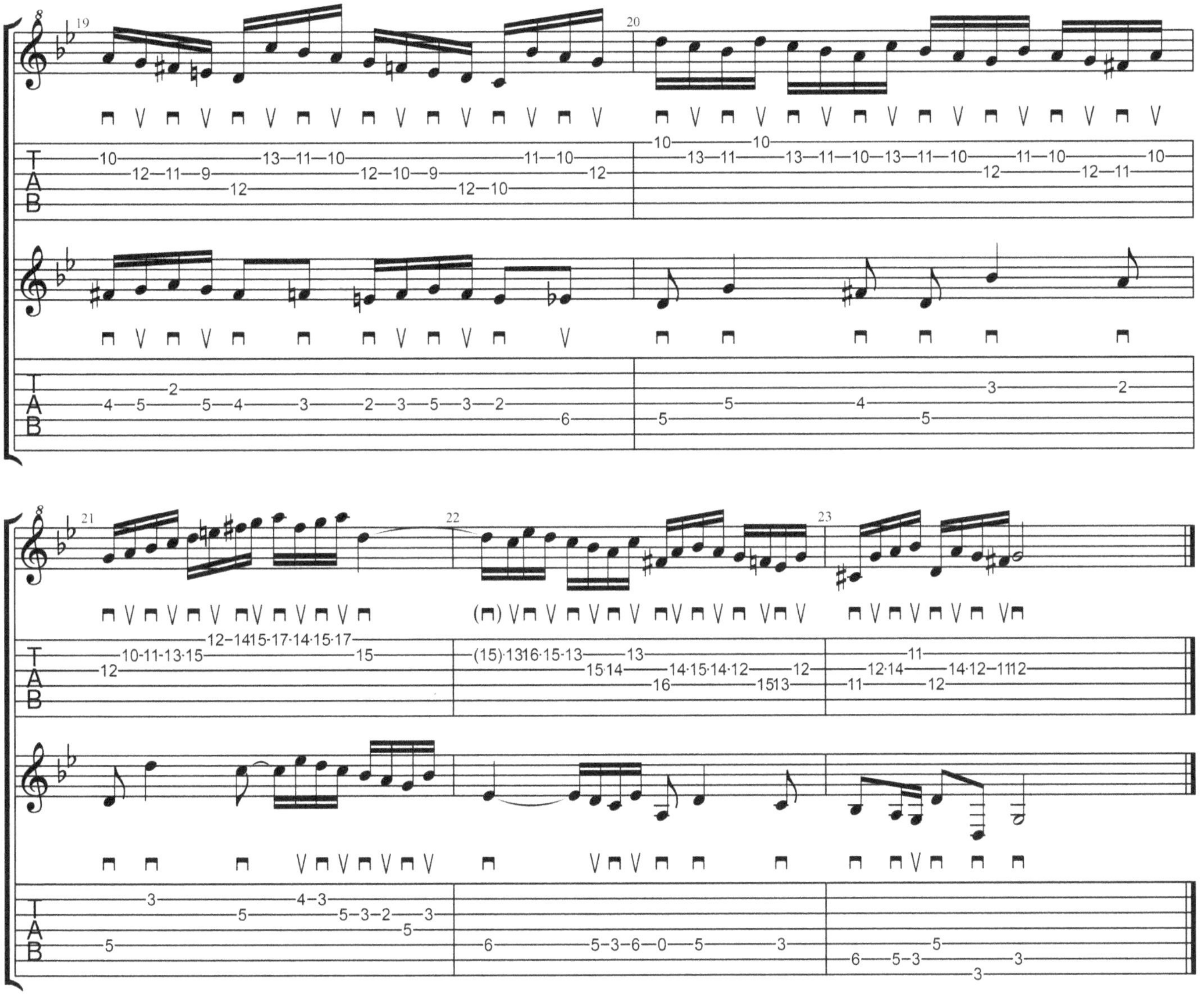

Invention Twelve in A Major

Invention Twelve might be my favourite in the set. The flowing arpeggios offer a real challenge when played at speed, but they're incredibly satisfying to work on.

We're back in compound time here, with a 12/8 time signature. Just as 9/8 relates to 3/4, 12/8 is essentially 4/4 with triplets on each beat. There are still four main pulses in each bar, but each beat contains three notes felt as an 1/8th note triplet. As you'll see, each 1/8th note is then often split into two 1/16ths but there are still four pulses in the bar which are phrased as 1/8th note accents.

To keep alternate picking consistent, I start each triplet with a downstroke. That way, any 1/16th note passages fall into a natural picking motion without having to adjust the rhythm or picking direction.

There are plenty of highlights in this piece, and I almost picked the alternating arpeggios between the two voices in bar seven. Instead, I've chosen to focus on bar thirteen. Here, we move from an F# arpeggio into B minor. It's a smooth transition if you use your middle finger to fret the 7th fret on the G string, which puts your index finger in position to catch the 7th fret on the E string straight after.

Example 16a:

Another highlight is the B Major arpeggio which spans 10 frets near the end of the piece. The trick here is making the position changes seamless. The listener shouldn't hear the mechanics, only the phrase. Start slowly and work up to speed.

Example 16b:

Here's the full Invention.

Example 16c:

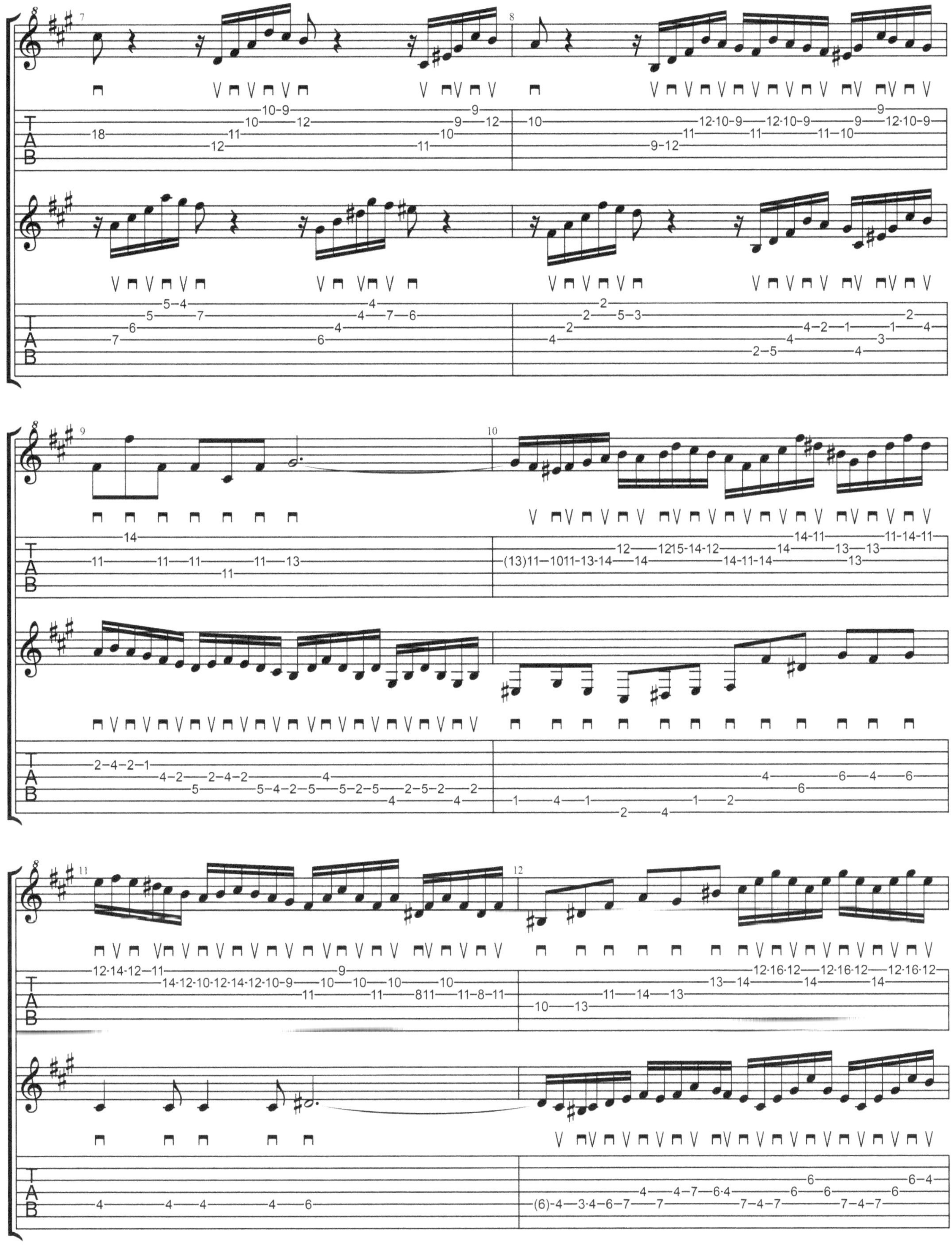

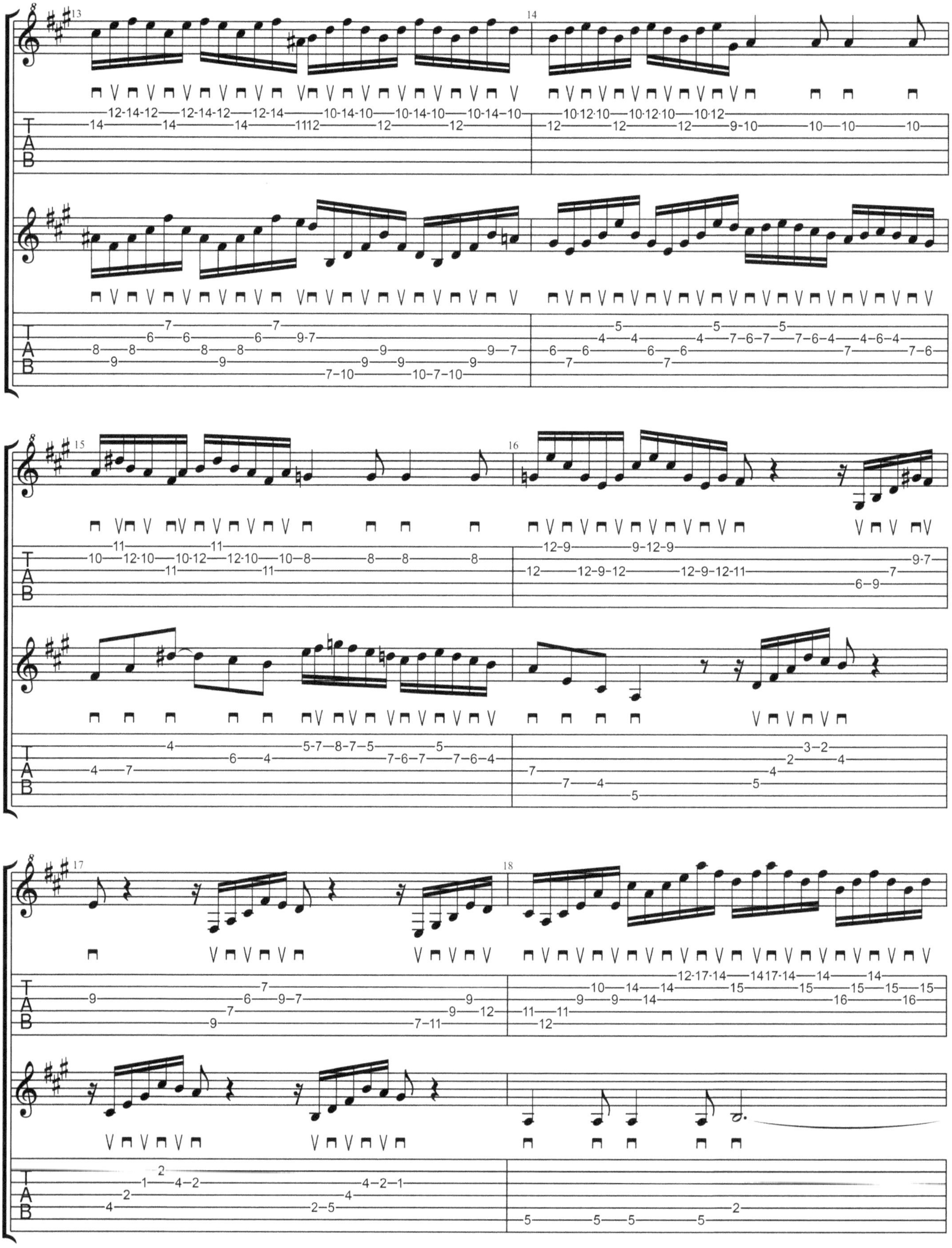

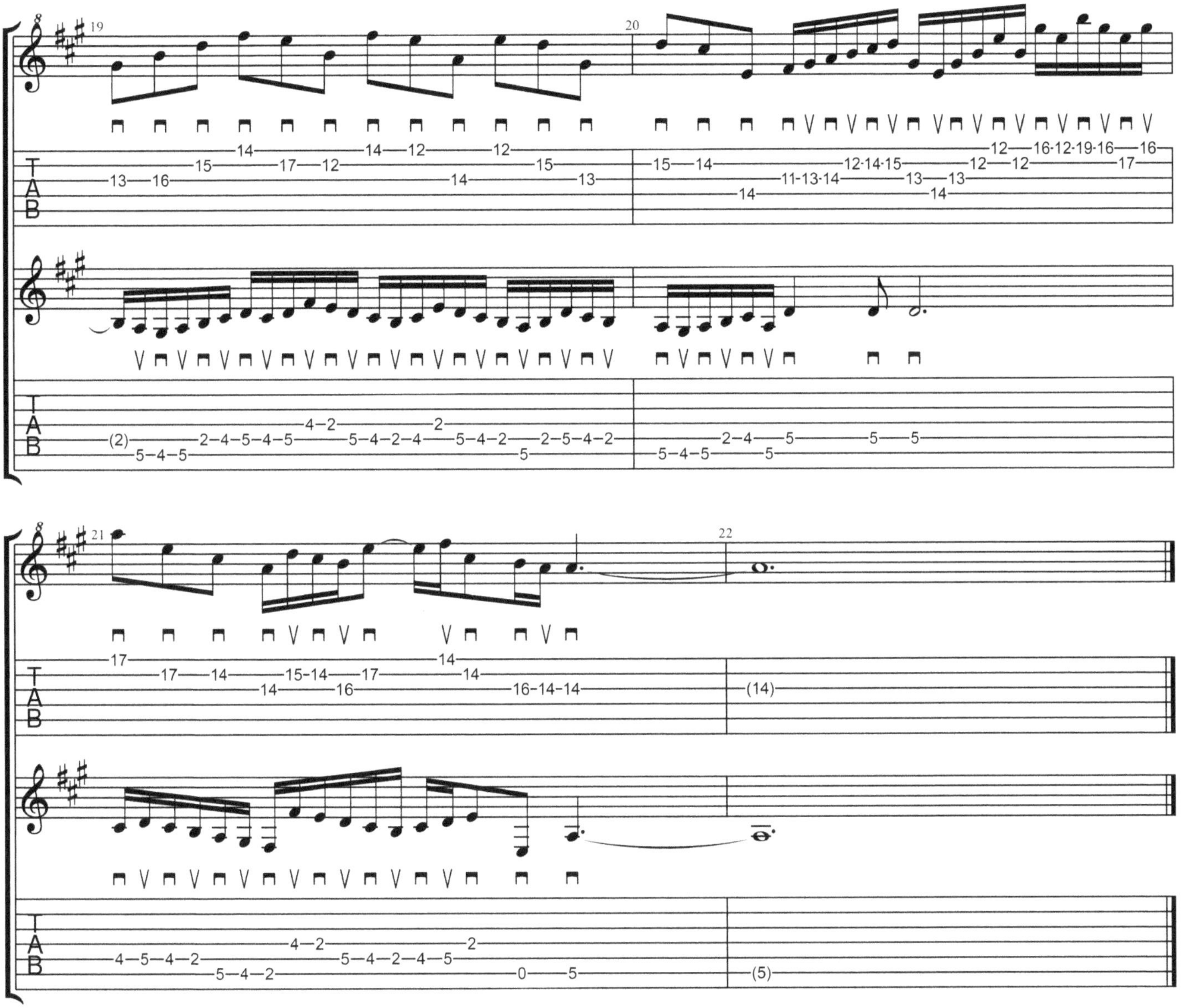
19
20
21
22
TAB

Invention Thirteen In A Minor

Invention Thirteen is another strong option if you're looking for a piece to study early on. The relaxed tempo makes it approachable while still offering some useful technical challenges.

It's particularly good at highlighting phrases that begin with upstrokes as many of the lines begin on the second 1/16th note of the beat, which means that your picking hand needs to be locked in. It might feel unfamiliar at first, but working on this kind of timing will really sharpen your picking control.

Bach also does something interesting by breaking up the arpeggios in a more creative way, giving the lines a musical shape that goes beyond simple up-and-down patterns.

Example 17a:

This is a great concept to explore. It can bring fresh energy to any arpeggio pattern and help you move away from the predictable up-and-down shapes we often fall back on. Here's an example that spans all six strings. We start with a C Major triad based around the E shape, then move into an F Major triad using the A shape.

Example 17b:

Here's the full Invention.

Example 17c:

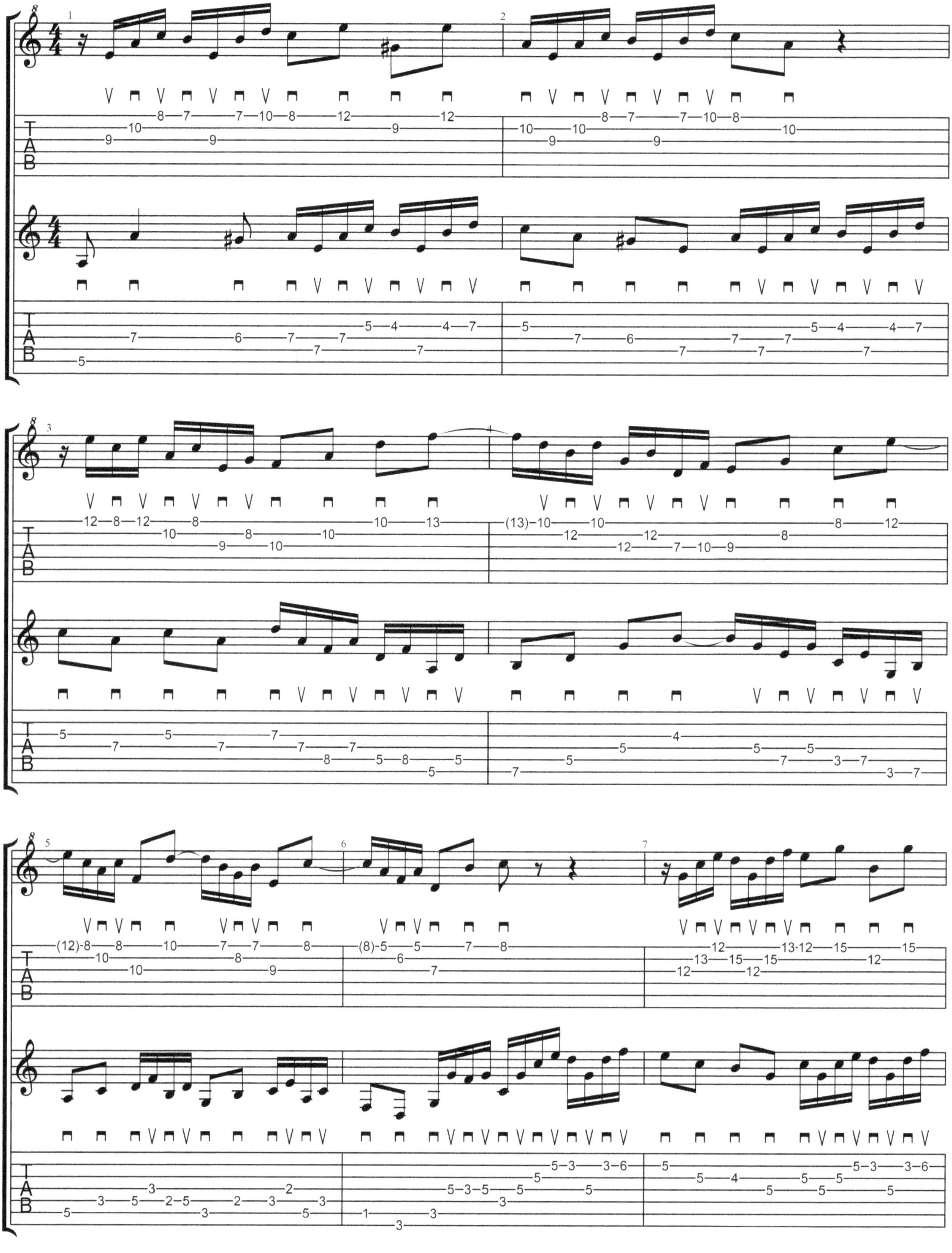

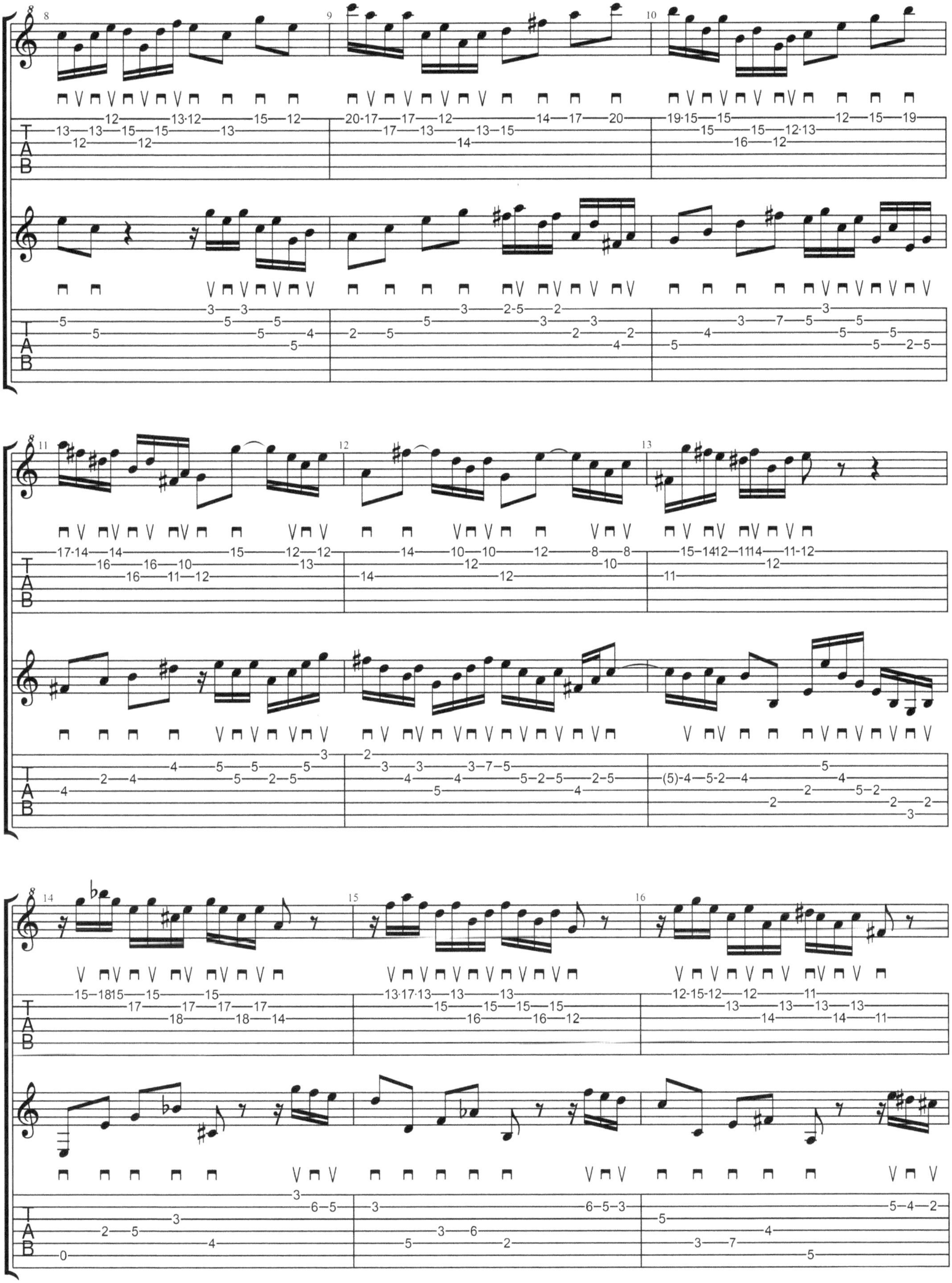

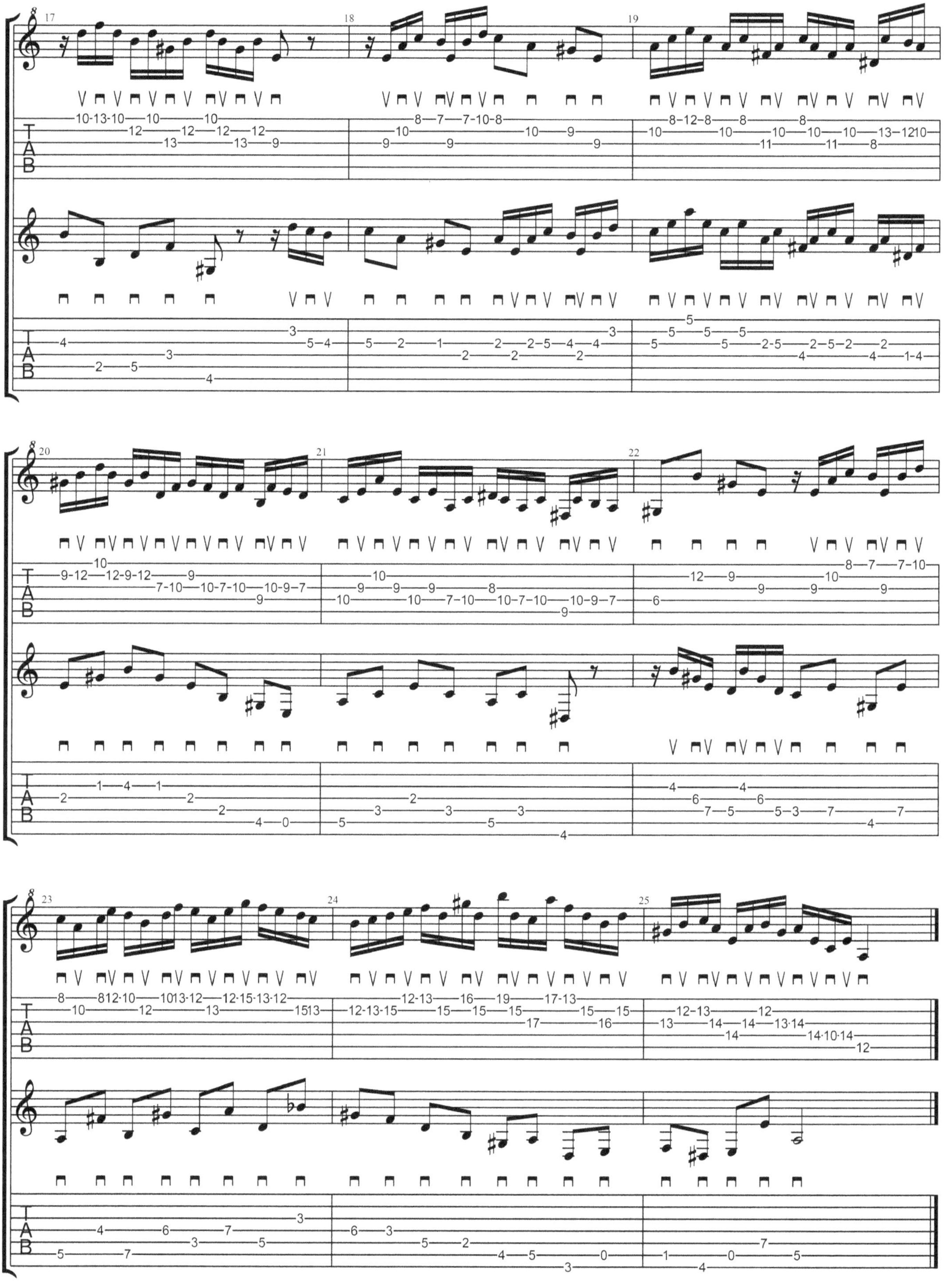

Invention Fourteen in Bb Major

This penultimate Invention is played at a slower tempo, but the inclusion of 1/32nd notes makes it a real test for your picking hand. To help with tone and picking consistency, I've arranged the faster runs so that they stay on a single string. Take this passage as an example.

Example 18a:

It's technically playable across strings, but very difficult to do so. Moving the phrase to a single string requires a few more shifts, but it makes the picking much more manageable.

Example 18b:

Take your time and ensure that both hands move cleanly through the position changes.

Example 18c:

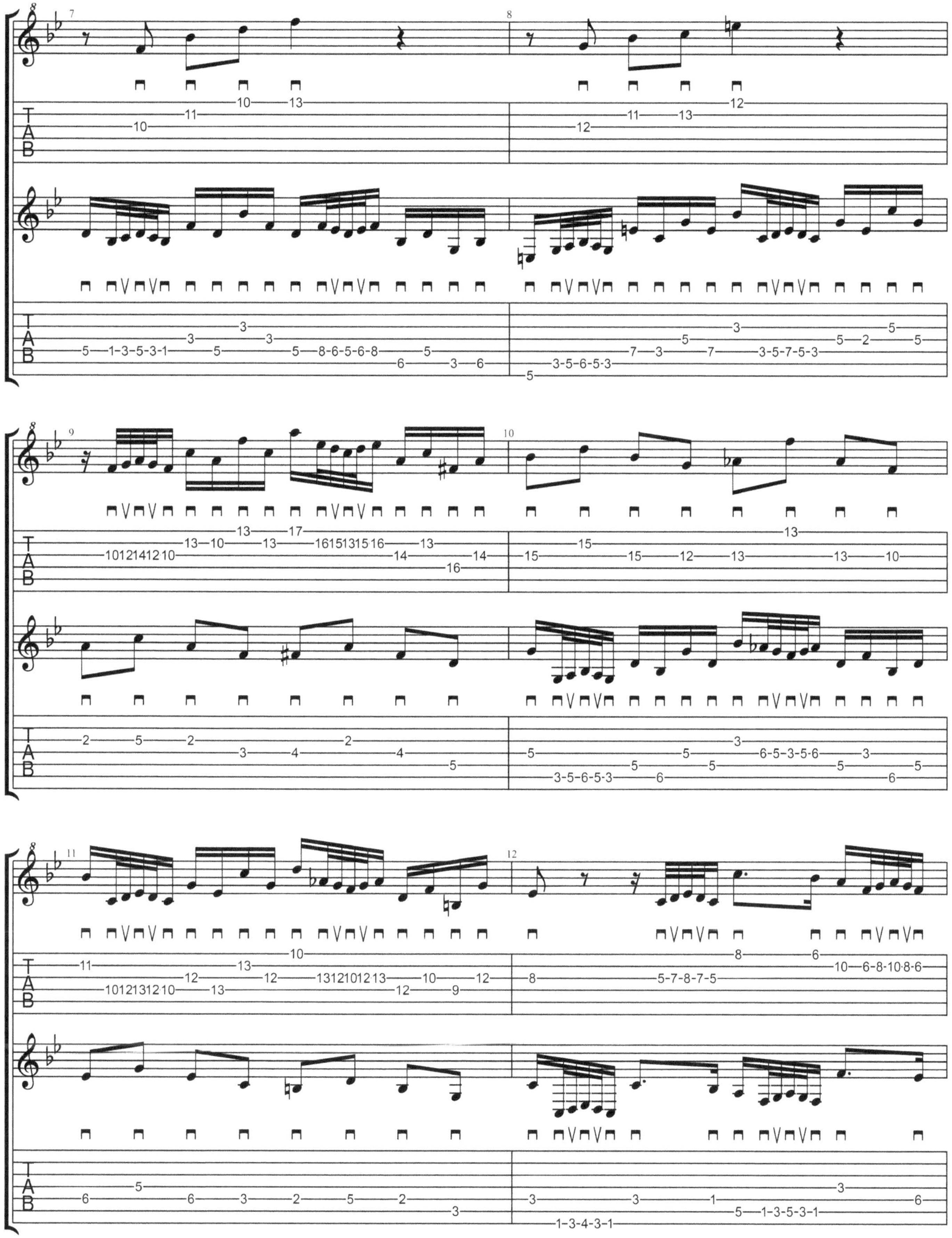

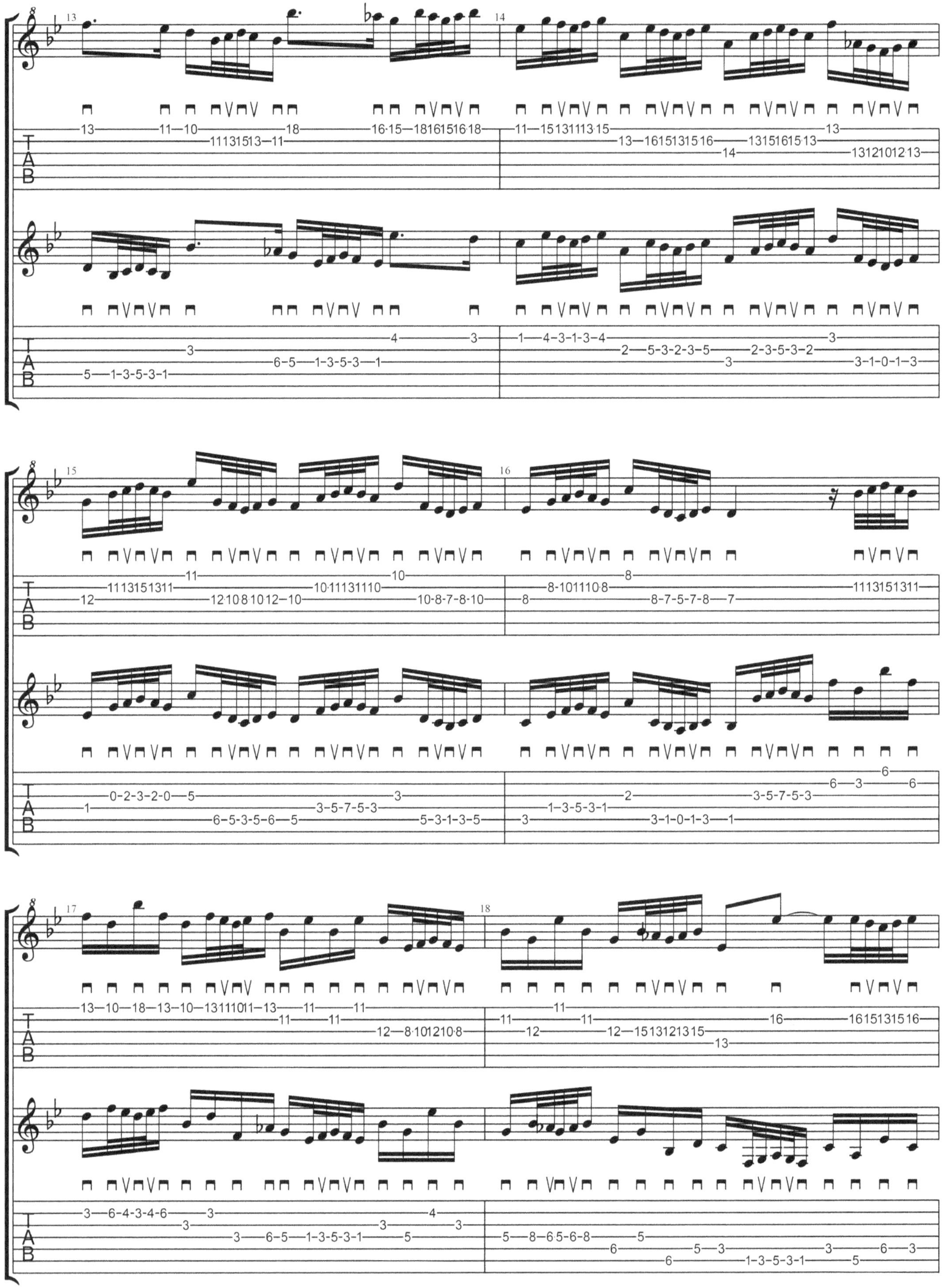

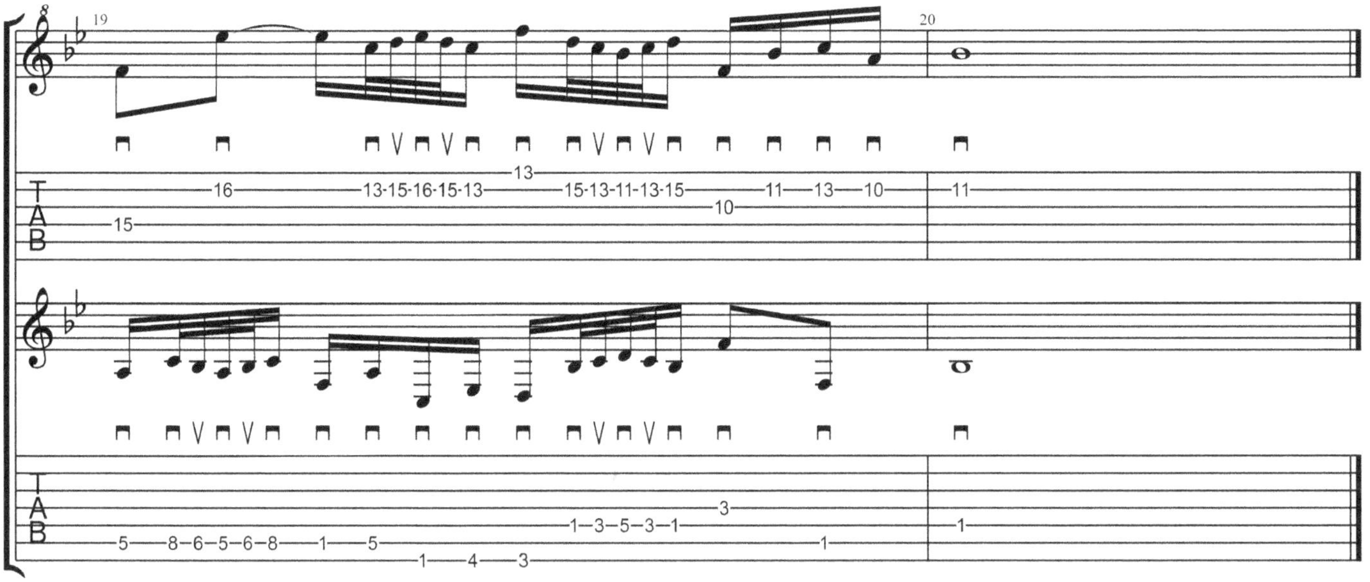
19
20
TAB
TAB

Invention Fifteen in B Minor

As with many of the minor key pieces, this Invention is more relaxed. You can think of it as a cooldown to round off the set.

There's a two-beat motif in this piece that I particularly enjoy. Bach reworks it in a few different ways as the Invention unfolds, keeping things interesting while staying rooted in a simple, effective idea.

Example 19a:

I think what makes this motif so engaging is the contrast. The first beat features a quick run of scale notes, while the second beat jumps out with a wider interval. To explore this further, this idea exaggerates those intervals to push the technique even further.

Example 19b:

Now let's finish with Invention Fifteen in full.

Example 19c:

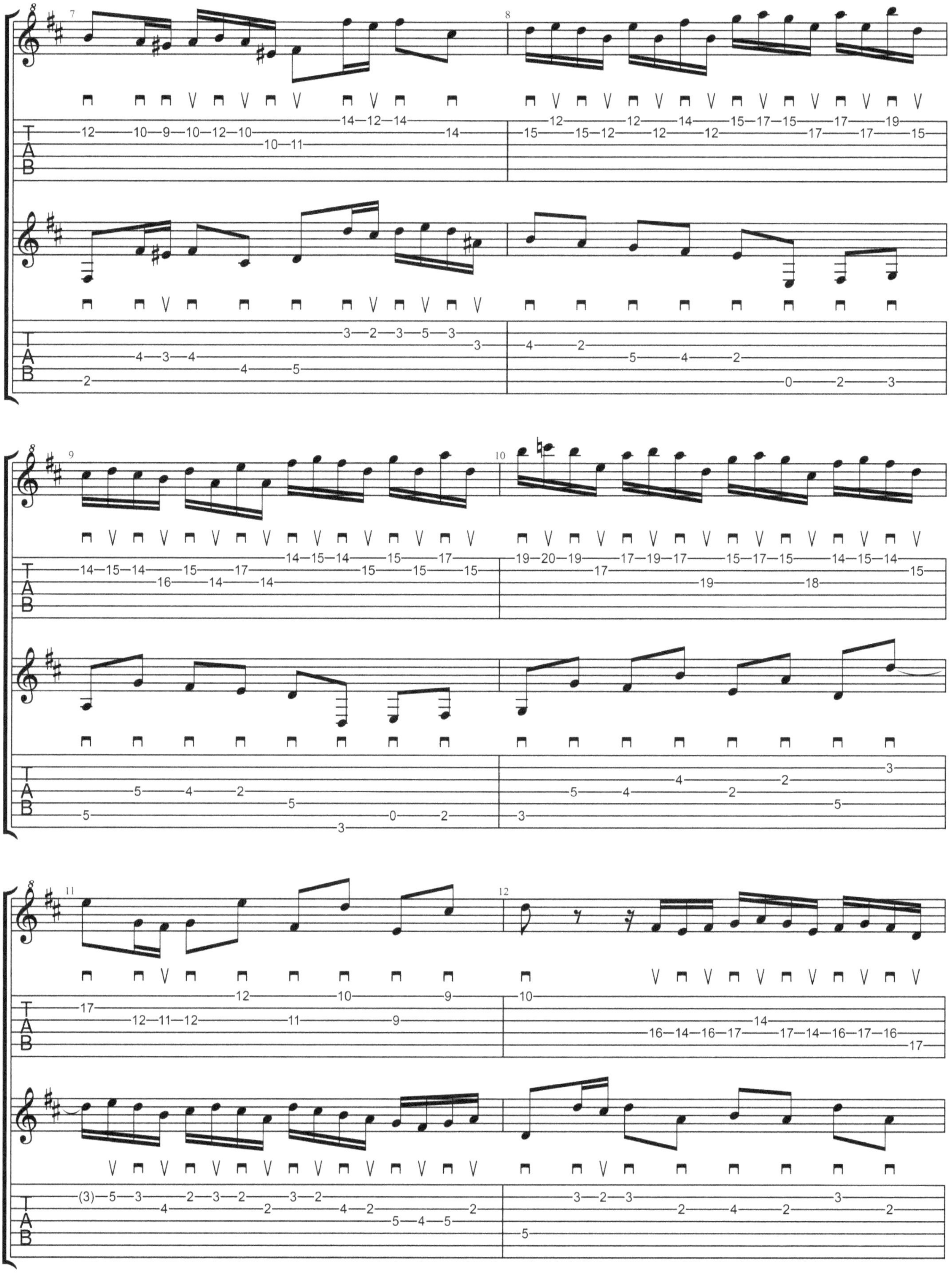

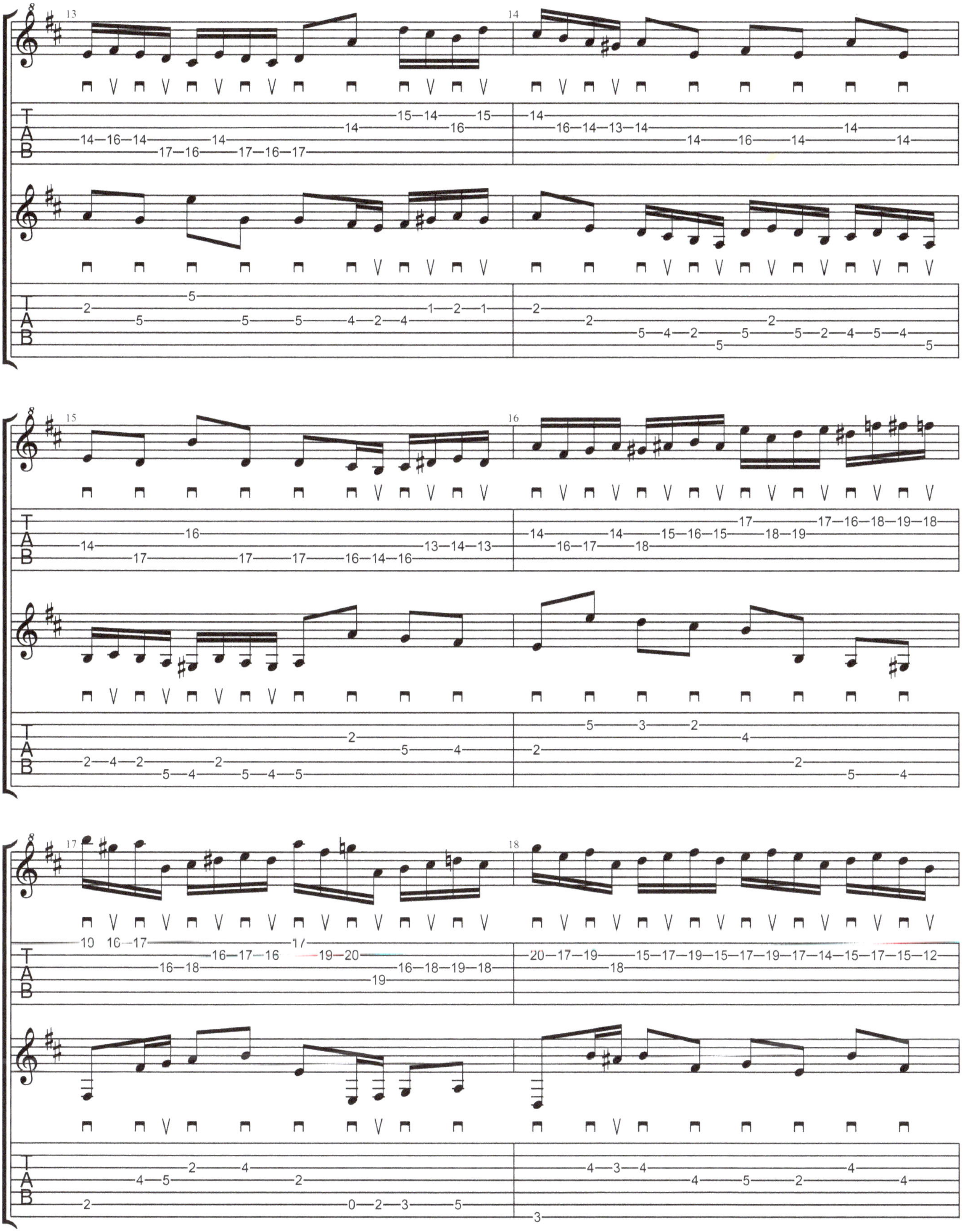

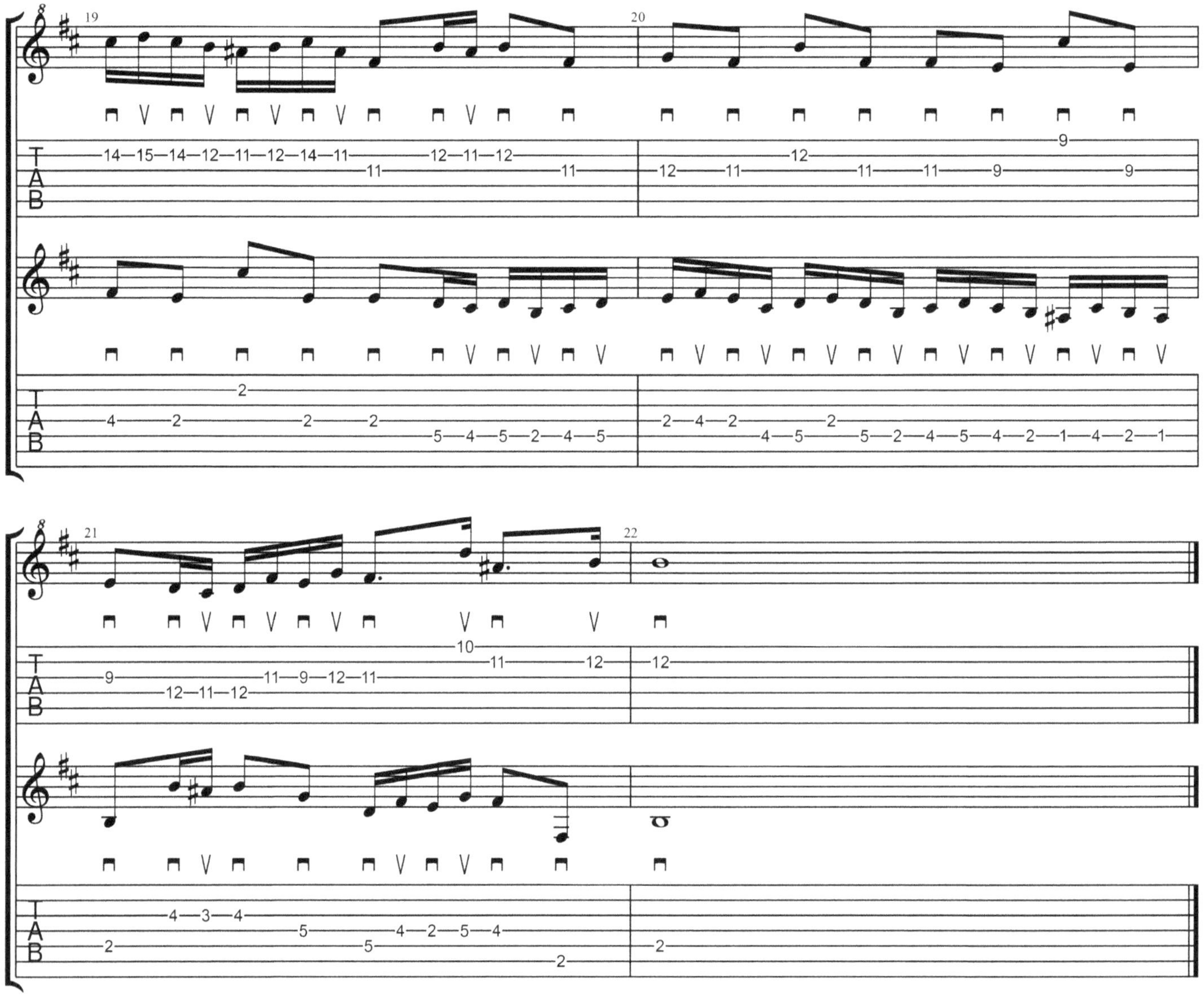
19
20
TAB
TAB
21
22
TAB
TAB

Conclusion

I hope that working through these Inventions has given you a deeper appreciation of Bach's music, as well as a solid technical workout on the guitar. The pieces may be short, but they're packed with musical content. They challenge your technique, develop your sense of harmony and melody, and help you understand how two independent voices can interact on the instrument.

You have encountered all of the key technical elements Bach weaves into the Inventions, meaning that your picking control will have improved, your rhythm will be more solid, and you'll have a clearer sense of how scales and harmony work when shared between two voices.

If you've made it through all 15, you've achieved something that not many guitarists take on, and even fewer complete.

From here, there are a few great directions you might want to explore.

If you enjoyed the contrapuntal nature of these pieces, take a look at Bach's Sinfonias (also known as the Three-Part Inventions). These are the natural next step. As the name suggests, they add a third voice. You could arrange them for three guitars, or work on them with a second player and get creative with how the lines are shared.

You might also enjoy exploring Bach's Lute Suites. These were written for an instrument with a lot in common with the guitar. A great place to start is the Lute Suite in E Minor, BWV 996, which includes a powerful Prelude and a beautifully flowing Allemande.

If you're keen to continue building your classical technique and get deeper into early music, try looking at works by composers like Scarlatti, Telemann, or Weiss. Much of their music transfers well to the guitar, and fingerstyle players in particular will find a lot to enjoy and learn from.

And if you've truly caught the Bach bug, consider studying the Well-Tempered Clavier. These keyboard works sit at the centre of Western music. They are complex and demanding, but even learning a single Prelude or Fugue will teach you a huge amount about harmony, voice leading, and musical structure.

The goal, always, is not just to play the notes, but to understand how they work. Ask yourself why a phrase sounds the way it does, how Bach moves between keys, and what makes each Invention unique.

Thank you for joining me on this journey. Keep practicing, stay curious, and continue exploring the music that inspires you.

Levi